Leadership will continue to be a hot issue in the twenty-first century. Larry Michael has taken a nineteenth-century pastoral hero and presented him as a contemporary model for Christian leaders today. In the process, we hear Spurgeon speak to many leadership issues in a challenging way that impacts us all. I highly recommend this book to all serious students of leadership!

> JOHN C. MAXWELL
> Founder, the INJOY Group

My great-grandfather came to Christ and was trained as a pastor through the ministry of Charles Spurgeon. He passed on to me many of Spurgeon's insights through his books and articles, which I treasure to this day. . . . Spurgeon's model of leadership has profoundly influenced my life and ministry. I'm thrilled that Larry Michael's wonderful and insightful new book will introduce a new generation to Spurgeon's model of leadership.

> RICK WARREN, AUTHOR
> *The Purpose-Driven Church*
> *The Purpose-Driven Life*

In every generation a few leaders emerge to set the pace and establish the standards for leadership. Charles Haddon Spurgeon was definitely one of those great leaders. And now Larry Michael, one of the true Spurgeon scholars of this day, brings together the qualities and traits that made Spurgeon an example for us in the twenty-first century. *Spurgeon on Leadership* is outstanding. Dr. Michael has truly written a book to be read by many and to be used in the classroom for years to come.

> THOM S. RAINER
> Dean, Billy Graham School of Missions, Evangelism, and Church Growth
> The Southern Baptist Theological Seminary
> Louisville, Kentucky

D0725744

Author Larry Michael knows Spurgeon like no other man in America. Every paragraph drips with enthusiasm for Spurgeon, and inside the pages are dozens of illustrations of what Spurgeon did, thought, and said. If you want to learn about Spurgeon, then read what Larry Michael has said about him.

ELMER L. TOWNS
Dean, School of Religion, Liberty University
Lynchburg, Virginia

In a day when leadership in the home, the church, and the nation is so weak and compromised, a book based on Spurgeon's biblical knowledge and pastoral experience on Christian leadership is both timely and crucial.

STEPHEN F. OLFORD
Chairman and Founder, The Stephen Olford Center for Biblical Preaching
Memphis, Tennessee

Larry Michael has chosen one of the greatest leaders in history, Charles Spurgeon, as a model for leaders and pastors today. Spurgeon was a true phenomenon in his day, fully one hundred years ahead of his time in building a megachurch. Every pastor and leader will be greatly blessed by this book.

JAMES MERRITT
Senior Pastor, First Baptist Church, Snellville, Georgia
Former President, Southern Baptist Convention

Here is a fresh approach to one of the towering figures in the history of the evangelical church. Larry Michael makes Spurgeon live again and shows us why we all have much to learn from the greatest master pastor since the Reformation.

TIMOTHY GEORGE
Dean, Beeson Divinity School, Samford University
Executive Editor, *Christianity Today*

Spurgeon on Leadership is an indispensable companion to the numerous works on Spurgeon the preacher. I strongly recommend . . . this volume by Larry Michael as it provides helpful mentoring material from the life of Spurgeon on the key aspect of the spiritual formation of a pastor.

DAVID COFFEY
General Secretary, Baptist Union of Great Britain (BUGB)
Vice President, Baptist World Alliance (BWA)

Dr. Michael writes with integrity. He has always exemplified good leadership and has desired to inspire others to high levels of quality leadership. To this end, he knows there is much to be learned from C. H. Spurgeon. . . . [T]his book . . . highlights the best qualities of leadership that Spurgeon lived and taught.

DAVID E. BEER
Pastor, Frinton Free Church, Essex, England
British Director, Purpose Driven Churches

SPURGEON
ON LEADERSHIP

UPDATED EDITION

SPURGEON
ON LEADERSHIP

Key Insights for Christian Leaders from the Prince of Preachers

LARRY J. MICHAEL

Kregel
Academic & Professional

Spurgeon on Leadership: Key Insights for Christian Leaders from the Prince of Preachers

© 2003, 2010 by Larry J. Michael

Updated chapters 5 and 13 with other minor changes throughout the book.

Published by Kregel Publications, a division of Kregel, Inc., 2450 Oak Industrial Dr. NE, Grand Rapids, MI 49505.

All rights reserved. No part of this book may be reproduced, stored in a retrieval system, or transmitted in any form or by any means—electronic, mechanical, photocopy, recording, or otherwise—without written permission of the publisher, except for brief quotations in printed reviews.

Scripture quotations marked NIV are from the *Holy Bible, New International Version*®. © 1973, 1978, 1984 by International Bible Society. Used by permission of Zondervan. All rights reserved.

Scripture quotations marked NKJV are from the *New King James Version*. © 1979, 1980, 1982, Thomas Nelson, Inc. Used by permission.

Scripture quotations marked KJV are from the King James Version of the Holy Bible.

ISBN 978-0-8254-3536-2

Printed in the United States of America
3 4 5 6 7 / 24 23 22 21 20 19 18 17 16

Remembering Christian leaders formative in my life:

Rev. David E. Beer (1938–2008)
Dr. Lewis A. Drummond (1926–2004)
Rev. Ralph A. Michael (1923–1999)
Dr. Stephen F. Olford (1918–2004)

CONTENTS

FOREWORD

Few people argue against the contention that the greatest pastor-evangelist of the British scene in the dynamic nineteenth century was Charles Haddon Spurgeon. His life and ministry present a model of what it means to be an outstanding pastor and leader.

Spurgeon came to the Metropolitan Tabernacle, as his church later became known, at the young age of nineteen. The first Sunday morning that he preached to the congregation that had gathered, only eighty people heard his message. By the time of his death thirty-seven years later, however, Spurgeon had been used of God to build the largest evangelical church in the world. His name is still a household word in many circles although he has been gone for more than a century. This fact not only speaks highly of Spurgeon's great preaching ability but also highlights his outstanding leadership on the London scene during the last half of the 1800s.

Those were dynamic days, to be sure. The British of the time reputedly were "notoriously religious." Still, the outstanding preaching and leadership ability that Spurgeon displayed gives us yet today a pattern of what it means to be an effective Christian leader.

In this new work, *Spurgeon on Leadership* by Dr. Larry Michael, the author has outlined and presented the basic leadership fundamentals and principles that Spurgeon incorporated so well into his life and ministry. This book covers the gamut of the aspects of leadership. Dr. Michael points out not merely the mechanics or psychology of what it means to be an influential leader but also important fundamentals such as Christian commitment and moral character. Moreover, he shows how Spurgeon demonstrated extreme courage and conviction for those principles and how, in the various controversies that surrounded his ministry, he rose to meet them with a genuine sense of Christian maturity and biblical fidelity. Michael also stresses important characteristics such as grasping a vision for the task and prioritizing one's ministry in both the setting and the context of pastoral compassion and leadership. He does not exclude the fact that leadership often entails suffering, and that was where Spurgeon truly ascended to the heights of leadership. Additionally, he offers good insight into the creativity and innovation that is demanded in leadership.

Self-evident from just a glance at this book is the fact that here are all of the essential ingredients of good leadership cast in the context of the fascinating life and ministry of the great London "prince of preachers." As the author has stated, "Leadership is a hot topic in many circles today." It has become obvious that many people in the ranks of Christian service—ministers and laypeople alike—grapple for an answer to the question of how to fulfill their vision and ministry and thus lead others in the service of Christ. This book will be of tremendous help in that quest. I highly commend it to anyone who is interested in making an impact for Christ in their day and generation. Dr. Michael has produced a superb work; it will unquestionably make a lasting contribution to many lives.

—LEWIS A. DRUMMOND

ACKNOWLEDGMENTS

The scope of this project was larger than I first imagined it would be. Undoubtedly, it would not have become a reality without the support and encouragement of others in the journey.

Dr. Lewis Drummond—my mentor in academia, my supervisor in the Ph.D. program, my advocate, my colleague in teaching, my friend—contributed much to this writing. The course we cotaught at Beeson Divinity School, titled "Spurgeon on Leadership," was the inspiration and germination for this book. I appreciated so much Dr. Drummond's foreword, and the love for Spurgeon that he has nourished in my life. Many blessings be upon him and his dear wife Betty.

I appreciate Dr. Timothy George and the staff of Beeson Divinity School (Samford University, Birmingham, Alabama) for the opportunity to teach as an adjunct professor over the past eight years. That discipline was a stimulus that helped to hone academic skills and inform my thought processes in the area of leadership.

My church family at "Friendly" First Baptist Church, in Clanton, Alabama, provided a basis of love and support that encouraged me in my writing.

Leading an active church meant that time for writing came mostly at disciplined intervals. But, serving a wonderful congregation made the task more rewarding, and the ministry provided opportunities for application of Spurgeon's principles.

I was fortunate to be raised in a Christian family, my father and mother, Rev. and Mrs. Ralph Michael, instilling in me godly values and the example of leadership.

My children, Ashley, Kent, and Graham, inspired me, kept me balanced, and provided comic relief in the inevitable stress of it all. They, along with my dear Mary Ann, urged me toward the goal every step of the way.

Finally the Lord Jesus Christ be praised. He converts our weaknesses into strengths, and turns our possibilities into realities. The ultimate Leader enables us to become leaders for the great purpose of participating in His Kingdom's work on this earth. And that, after all, is what makes it all worthwhile.

INTRODUCTION

One of the universal cravings of our time is a hunger for
compelling and creative leadership.[1]

Leadership is a hot topic in many circles today, including among the heads of both religious and secular organizations. Among evangelical Christians, one of the names most recognized as a Christian leader is Charles H. Spurgeon. Perhaps no leader had a greater impact on the evangelical world in the nineteenth century than Spurgeon. He served as the pastor of the first megachurch, the Metropolitan Tabernacle in London, for more than thirty-seven years, preaching to more than five thousand worshipers every Sunday. His sermons were in great demand, most of them were published weekly, and they are still available today.

Spurgeon wrote dozens of books that remain in print and continue to inspire evangelicals. He began a college for the training of pastors, and it currently has the distinction of being the largest evangelical institution for theological training in Europe. He founded an orphanage for homeless children that rivaled that of the great George Müller. His philanthropies are legendary and include more than twenty-five different organizations ranging from "The Ladies Maternal Society" to "The Metropolitan Tabernacle Poor Minister's Clothing Society." He provided great pastoral leadership in many enterprises that advanced education, provided benevolent relief, and offered practical innovations in ministry, thereby promoting the gospel of Jesus Christ.

His influence was felt in not only the Christian world but also the social and political realms of Victorian England. Among those who frequented his church and valued his friendship were prime ministers and future U.S. presidents. At the same time, he was known for his ability to communicate with the common person. He embodied a unique style of leadership that influenced the lives of many different kinds of people. Today, Spurgeon is still read and quoted by many evangelical Christian leaders, a fact that demonstrates his enduring popularity as a pastoral figure.

This book features Spurgeon's leadership principles, methods, teachings, and practical innovations—relevant to both pastors and Christian lay leaders—all of which can be applied equally well in the pulpit, in the classroom, or for personal edification. Publishers have offered the secular world books such as *Lincoln on Leadership* and *Churchill on Leadership,* which focused on political leaders. Here now is offered to the religious community *Spurgeon on Leadership.* This book lets Spurgeon speak to Christian issues that are identifiable in the current socio-politico-religious setting. It makes practical applications, using some contemporary leaders and the author's personal experience in ministry. It is offered to readers with the hope that those who are seeking to grow in their leadership will learn Christian principles that have withstood the test of time.

PART ONE

The Leader for All Seasons

1

COMPETENCE

Developing and Demonstrating Leadership

Go forward. Go forward in personal attainments, forward in
gifts and in grace, forward in fitness for the work, and forward
in conformity to the image of Jesus.[1]

Charles Haddon Spurgeon was amazingly competent in ministry, excelling in so many different areas of leadership that it almost boggles the mind when one considers the immense contribution he made as a Christian leader. His level of accomplishment is even more astonishing in light of the fact that he was largely self-taught, having had no formal training beyond secondary schooling. This fact does not mean, however, that Spurgeon eschewed the value of education. At one point, in his first pastorate at Waterbeach, the young pastor considered the possibility of theological training. Stepney College (later to become Regents Park College at Oxford University) made overtures to him, and the principal sought an interview immediately. He scheduled a meeting with Spurgeon at a particular place. Upon their independent arrivals, however, a servant girl unknowingly sent the two men to two different rooms, and each man thought that the other one had not arrived. They both departed after waiting for some time; subsequently, the desired meeting did not occur.

Spurgeon interpreted this mishap as one signal that he should not pursue formal theological training. In addition, he received what he perceived to be a direct message from God while walking across a village common where he was guest speaker at a local lay preachers' association. Spurgeon wrote,

> In the midst of the Common I was startled by what seemed a loud voice, but which may have been a singular illusion. Whichever it

was, the impression was vivid to an intense degree; I seemed very distinctly to hear the words, "Seekest thou great things for thyself? Seek them not!" This led me to look at my position from another point of view, and to challenge my motives and intentions.[2]

Spurgeon interpreted this experience as a reinforcement of his decision not to seek theological training at that time. The ministry at Waterbeach had increased to the extent of 450 regular worshipers, and Spurgeon believed that his first commitment was to tend the flock to which God had called him. Subsequent events, including his call to London, reinforced Spurgeon's pursuit of self-study rather than formal training at theological college.

Commitment to Personal Education

Spurgeon's decision not to pursue formal theological training, however, did not deter him from doggedly pursuing personal education. He read voraciously, testifying that he completed three to five books per week. Spurgeon's brother wrote about him,

> He never did anything else but study. I kept rabbits, chickens, and pigs, and a horse; he kept to books. While I was busy here and there, meddling with anything and everything that a boy could touch, he kept to books, and could not be kept away from study. . . . He made such progress in his studies that I am sure there were few young men that were his equals and I do not know any that were his superiors.[3]

Because of Spurgeon's positive obsession with books, he became so widely versed that he equaled, if not surpassed, many of his ministerial peers in theological development and other disciplines. He studied not only the Bible but also science, history, literature, and astronomy. Works on these subjects as well as religious books comprised his twelve thousand-volume personal library.

Eventually, Spurgeon's insatiable appetite for reading inspired him to critique the latest theological and religious books, reviewing them regularly for the readers of his church magazine, *The Sword and the Trowel*. In addition, he wrote a book titled *Commenting and Commentaries* analyzing critically all of the commentaries of his day. In retrospect, some historians have observed that when Spurgeon became involved in some notable religious controversies, theological training might have broadened his ministerial graces through the rigors of classroom instruction and interaction with other students. Regardless, one could not assume that the absence of formal training resulted in any disadvantages concerning his theological acumen. Spurgeon's self-discipline and determination to continue his personal studies enabled him to keep abreast of developments and trends that were instructive for his ever-expanding ministry.

Training Pastors

Spurgeon's personal commitment to education instilled within him a desire to provide practical training for pastors. This desire led him to found The Pastors' College, which was named not for him but for the ministers who would receive instruction to benefit them in their local pastorates. He believed that competence in ministry was necessary for leaders to make progress in their service to Christ.

The leader today must be committed to ministerial competence. Education, personal charisma, and natural abilities might achieve a short-lived following, but there is no substitute for the continued development of spiritual gifts and practical skills for the work of the ministry. Certainly God is a partner in the process, as recorded in Ephesians 2:10: "We are God's workmanship, created in Christ Jesus to do good works, which God prepared in advance for us to do" (NIV). Although God endows us with certain spiritual gifts, it is our responsibility to become equipped and trained for the work that He calls us to do.

Many leaders are well-intentioned, but they are not resolved in following through with their desire to improve their skills. Leroy Eims writes, "Good intentions can't replace good performance. Leaders must be competent in the job God has given them to do."[4] Or, as the adage goes, "An ocean of intention is not worth as much as one drop of action." No intention will ever match the determined action that one takes in developing one's skills in the pursuit of excellence in leadership. Spurgeon mentored his many young students with the following counsel:

> We ought to increase our capital stock. Are all the young brethren doing that? Are you increasing in gift and capacity? My brethren, do not neglect yourselves. I observe that some brethren grow, and others stand still, dwarfed and stunted. . . . The most needful and profitable labour is that which we spend upon our own mental and spiritual improvement.[5]

Steps to Personal Development

How does one become competent as a leader? Does it just happen by itself? Some people erroneously assume that leaders are born that way, that is, their leadership is natural, something that they didn't acquire from anyone. Even in Christian circles, the temptation exists to surmise that leadership is simply a spiritual gift and nothing more. It is undoubtedly more correct to say that leadership is a learned discipline. John Maxwell, a renowned leader of Christian leaders, addressed the issue:

> That question is asked a lot, "Are leaders born?" My answer is always the same, "Of course they are. So are non-leaders. We're all born." What they really are asking is, "Are some people born with gifts of leadership? Are there just natural leaders?" . . . There are people who are born with leadership gifts who have the potential to become 10s, and 10 is tops. But those individuals, unless they cultivate leadership and develop and train and learn and read and discipline themselves, will never be the leaders they could be. The flip side is that there is no question in my mind that you CAN learn to lead if you do NOT have those natural leadership gifts.[6]

Learning Leadership

Leadership does not belong exclusively to those who are so-called "natural" leaders. You could put it this way: "The best leadership is that which is *acquired*, not that which is *sired*." Notable examples exist of great leaders, from royal families downward, who have given birth to heirs who did not achieve the same level of leadership as their parents. In those instances, it becomes apparent that more than genes determines the extent of one's leadership capabilities.

Spurgeon did not countenance the notion that leaders were thus gifted and did not need training. He recognized the need for ministers to become competent in their roles as pastors and leaders. In one of his weekly lectures to his students at The Pastors' College, he spoke on the subject of "The Necessity of Ministerial Progress."[7] He lamented the squandering of opportunity by some ministers who had God-given potential: "Alas! too many young men destroy our hopes; they are extravagant in their expenses, make an unfortunate marriage, fall into ill humours, wander after novel opinions, give way to laziness and self-indulgence, or in some other way fail to improve themselves."[8] Spurgeon's words reveal his belief that a leader must be willing to apply himself to become a more effective leader.

What are the elements that demonstrate that a Christian leader has "skilled competence?"

Communication

Leaders must communicate to lead effectively. It doesn't matter if you have a vision and know where God is leading you. If you can't communicate it to your followers, you will fail to accomplish your goals.

What are some of the barriers to effective communication? Kenneth Gangel addresses some of these barriers in his instructive book for pastoral shepherds *Feeding and Leading.*[9] He mentions barriers of perception that might color your thinking. One's lack of self-esteem might restrict communication, inhibiting one's leadership. Also, one might sense a hierarchical barrier with the differences in status between leader and layperson. Personality clashes might prohibit one's connecting with followers. And polarization might occur because of different value systems.

Gangel continues that a leader must learn to connect with his followers, especially through preaching and teaching in the pastoral context. He must use all of his social skills to get his message across. In the overall organization, the leader must keep people informed adequately. Don't bypass appropriate channels. Give timely, accurate, appropriate information to motivate your followers. And don't fail to seek feedback.[10]

Increasing Communication Effectiveness

How does one become a better communicator? Be current. Know what's going on in the world. Study other speakers. Note the way in which they communicate their message. Connect and identify with your hearers. Be passionate about your subject.

Spurgeon gave several admonitions regarding communication, especially with preaching in mind. He issued the following four directives.

1. *Cultivate a clear style.* Spurgeon wrote, "When a man does not make me understand what he means, it is because he does not himself know what he

means."[11] He decried the pseudointellectuals of his day, who sought to impress their hearers with their depth. With some humor, he exclaimed, "I believe that many 'deep' preachers are simply so because they are like dry wells with nothing whatever in them, except decaying leaves, a few stones, and perhaps a dead cat or two."[12] Spurgeon believed that the speaker should simplify his message for all persons. "It is not enough to be so plain that you can be understood, you must speak so that you cannot be misunderstood."[13]

2. *Cultivate a cogent style.* Spurgeon taught his students to be passionate about their subject. "Our speech must be forceful. Some imagine that this consists in speaking loudly, but I can assure them they are in error. Nonsense does not improve by being bellowed. . . . Let us be forcible by reason of the excellence of our matter, and the energy of spirit which we throw into the delivery of it."[14]

3. *Cultivate naturalness.* Spurgeon lamented speakers whose goal was to entertain rather than inform their hearers. "I hope we have foresworn the tricks of professional orators, the strain for effect, the studied climax, the pre-arranged pause, the theatric strut, the mouthing of words, and I know not what besides, which you may see in certain pompous divines who still survive upon the face of the earth . . . may a living, natural, simple way of talking out the gospel be learned by us all."[15]

4. *Cultivate persuasiveness.* Spurgeon admired speakers who could connect personally with each hearer, "preachers who in their sermons seem to take their hearers one by one by the button-hole, and drive the truth right into their souls."[16] He encouraged preachers to adapt themselves to different situations. "Suit yourselves to your audiences. . . . The greatest master of oratory . . . is able to address any class of people in a manner suitable to their condition, and likely to touch their hearts."[17]

Spurgeon was well known for his special gift of communication, notably in his preaching. But, beyond that, he sought to be put into practice the instruction he gave his students lest he should be misunderstood in his efforts to share the message of the gospel of Christ.

Equipping the Saints

In addition to effective communication, a Christian leader demonstrates his competence by his ability to train laypeople for ministry. The apostle Paul wrote to the Ephesians that leaders are to equip the saints for the work of the ministry (Eph. 4:12). The leader must demonstrate competence in empowering others for service to Christ. Maxwell wrote, "The growth and development of other leaders is the highest calling of leadership."[18] Spurgeon saw this task as essential for the pastor:

> To do the Lord's work must be as necessary as food to us. His Father's work is that in which we also are engaged, and we cannot do better than imitate our Lord. Tell me, then, how Jesus set about it. Did He set about it by arranging to build a huge Tabernacle, or by organizing a monster Conference, or by publishing a great book, or by sounding a trumpet before Him in any other form? Did He aim at something great, and altogether out of the common line of service? Did He bid high for popularity, and wear Himself out by an exhausting sensationalism? No; He called disciples to Him one by one, and instructed each one with patient care.[19]

Sharing Ministry

The temptation for some leaders is to attempt to do all of the work of the ministry themselves. Because of busywork, administration, and other positional responsibilities, they might fail to delegate tasks or train others to assist in the ministry. A leader must be intentional in developing other leaders. The famous rubber baron, Harvey S. Firestone, aptly stated, "It is only as we develop others that we permanently succeed." Pastors and other Christian leaders were not called to do all of the work in the church. Andrew Carnegie was correct: "No man will make a great leader who wants to do it all himself, or to get all the credit for doing it." The leader's responsibility is to develop other leaders.

Spurgeon depended on the elders of the Metropolitan Tabernacle to conduct much of the business of the church. They were heavily involved in both administration and the financial affairs of the congregation. Charles also brought his brother James on staff to assist in the great demand of pastoral responsibilities. Even then, ongoing ministries were led and organized totally through the lay leaders of the church. On-the-job training was an essential part of the commitment to the ministry.

Developing Leaders Around You

A leader's ability to develop those around him will ultimately determine the outcome of his leadership. In the Christian context, I define *pastoral leadership* as "the *empowering* of laypersons to accomplish the mission of Christ through the local church." To empower people, we must mobilize them for ministry. We must seek to involve people, delegating areas of service that will multiply our own effectiveness. Such people must be unleashed and given the freedom to develop their particular ministries in the context of the local fellowship. Many people will have to be challenged to step out of their comfort zones, to leave their pews and take up their responsibilities. Just like rubber bands, people have to be stretched to be effective. Far too much complacency exists in the typical congregation. They will let the pastor do it all if he so desires. And, unfortunately, that happens too often. Equipping members has to go farther than printing in the bulletin that the pastor is Brother So-and-so, and that the ministers are the Congregation.

How does one become an equipper? First, you must be committed to *study* leadership (read, think, be creative). In addition to private study, you should attend seminars that give practical help. Second, learn all about your organization (read the church constitution/bylaws!). Third, commit to training others under your leadership. Fourth, concentrate on the laypeople who are willing to be trained, and follow through with your training. Finally, don't be afraid to risk giving away some of your job (don't do what you don't need to do). When you are faced with a responsibility or task, ask yourself, "Is this something I must do, or can I delegate it?"

Effectiveness in Ministry

A leader's competence is determined by communication skills and the ability to equip other leaders. A Christian leader must also demonstrate effectiveness in personal ministry. Leadership is *earned* as well as learned. A leader garners some influence simply because of his position, but increased influence comes when one gives evidence of effectiveness in personal ministry. Spurgeon wrote,

> We are *ministers*. The word has a very respectable sound. To be a minister is the aspiration of many a youth. Perhaps, if the word

were otherwise rendered, their ambition might cool. Ministers are servants; they are not guests, but waiters; not landlords, but labourers.[20]

Throughout his life, Spurgeon maintained his commitment to engage in personal ministry, setting aside specific times for interaction/counseling with his members.

Example in Ministry

An effective leader knows his gifts and abilities and uses them. Of necessity, you incarnate what you want to teach others. If you are a pastor and expect laypersons to become adept in the ministry of pastoral care, you, as a leader, must set the example. If you want your members to follow your leadership in ministry, they need to know that you are involved in personal evangelism, that you regularly make ministry visits, and that you're not above visiting the hospital. Some clergy today exhibit a stifling attitude of professionalism, relegating *all* ministry to other staff or laypeople.

Indeed, some Christian pastors have abdicated their personal ministry responsibilities altogether. One never attains the luxury of ministerial absenteeism in Christian leadership. It might be easy to "hang out" in the office, sipping that leisurely cup of coffee and enjoying the comforts that surround you. But, as John le Carré wrote, "A desk is a dangerous place from which to watch the world."[21] One must be "out there," demonstrating effectiveness in shepherding and nurturing the flock. The pastor has been anointed by God to lead the sheep, but such anointing is not automatic. Trust and "followership" must be earned. Spurgeon instructed his students, "Brethren, let us heartily love all whom Jesus loves. Cherish the tried and suffering. Visit the fatherless and the widow. Care for the faint and the feeble. Bear with the melancholy and despondent. Be mindful of all parts of the household, and thus shall you be a good steward."[22]

Increasing One's Ministry

How does a leader become more effective in ministry? Set priorities, work your priorities, and follow through. Do ministry!

Spurgeon admonished, "Labour to be alive in all your duties."[23] He was not afraid of hard work and often pushed himself to the limit in his responsibilities. He once declared, "I like Adam Clarke's precept: 'Kill yourselves with work, and then pray yourselves alive again.'"[24] Like Spurgeon, a leader needs to be passionate about the ministry that God has given him.

Do *more* than is expected. Some leaders today are so afraid of burnout that they seem to be conducting skeletal ministry, doing the minimal amount to get by. Other ministers are trying to do it all by themselves, not willing to bring others alongside and train them for ministry. A word to the wise: *never minister alone* (take someone along/train them). In this way, you multiply your ministry, and your leadership becomes "caught" as well as "taught."

People Oriented

The competence of a Christian leader depends on clear communication, concerted equipping of the saints, and ministerial effectiveness. Competence in leadership also depends on one's skills in relating to people. People buy into *you* before they buy into your leadership. You might be the most gifted leader in the world, but if you are not people oriented, your leadership will be limited. A good question to ask is, "Am I building people, or am I just building my own dream and using people to do it?" In God's work, we must invest ourselves in people; they are our greatest investment. A leader must make the extra effort to get to know his people.

I heard about a minister of music who requested an advance picture of the choir at the prospective church where he was to interview for a position. Upon arrival, he knew all of the names of the choir members, and his effort greatly impressed the church.

As Christian ministers, we are in the people business. Therefore, put people first (ahead of programs). In your leadership, you want to *add value* to people's lives. Continue to work to develop relationships (connect with people). As Jesus exemplified, put what's best for others ahead of yourself. *Always* make time for people. Be available and approachable. Allow for the unexpected. Seek to bring people together, uniting them in the cause of Christ.

Caring About People

Spurgeon issued this challenge regarding the people who are under one's leadership: "Look to the interests of all who are in Christ Jesus, and let them all be as dear to you as your own children. . . . Our Lord would have us thus identify ourselves with His holy business; and especially, He would have us love His chosen. We, beyond all others, should lay down our lives for the brethren."[25]

How can a leader become more people oriented? Care, care, care about people! The familiar saying is true: "People do not care how much you know until they know how much you care." Love and accept people as they are. Give people your E.A.R. (encouragement, appreciation, and recognition). Make heroes of your people. Admit your mistakes; be vulnerable. And always seek to reach people for Christ. Spurgeon believed that this attitude shows our greatest love for people: "I hope it will never get to be your notion that only a certain class of preachers can be soul-winners. Every preacher should labour to be the means of saving his hearers. The truest reward of our life-work is to bring dead souls to life."[26]

Goal Oriented

The competent leader communicates effectively, empowers followers for ministry, gives evidence of personal ministry, and demonstrates good skills with people. In addition, the competent leader is goal oriented, continuing to look to the future. Some leaders get stuck in the past, always looking to the earlier glory days. Spurgeon showed an appreciation for the great ministers who had preceded him in London, but he never let it get in the way of what God was calling him to do. Spurgeon's first goal was to please his Lord: "Our chief end is to glorify God. We do not regard it as our first business to convert sinners, nor to edify saints; but to glorify God."[27]

The Priority of Evangelism

Spurgeon believed that a pastor who seeks to glorify God must have goals. He must have a strong commitment to evangelism, taking seriously Christ's commission to take the gospel to the ends of the earth (Matthew 28:19–20). Spurgeon was convinced that evangelism must be intentional—it must be a goal. "If we would win souls, we must act accordingly, and lay ourselves out to that end. Men do not catch fish without intending it, nor save sinners unless they aim at it."[28]

The pastor at the Metropolitan Tabernacle challenged his students at The Pastors' College to pursue their ministries actively: "Brethren, do something;

do something; DO SOMETHING. While committees waste their time over reso-
lutions, do something. While Societies and Unions are making constitutions,
let us win souls. Too often we discuss, and discuss, and discuss, while Satan
only laughs in his sleeve. It is time we had done planning, and sought something to plan."[29]

The Price of Success

The ministry offers no guarantees of success, but to the degree that one sets
goals and is determined to do whatever it takes, a leader will eventually see
positive results. Maxwell stated, "Ninety-five percent of achieving anything is
knowing what you want and paying the price to get it."[30] Goals give you direction, ensure progress, and bring accomplishment. You must ensure that you
have concrete, attainable objectives. Work smart, and finish the tasks you start.
(There are many great beginners but not many great finishers). Act on your
goals, and carry them through to the end.

How can a leader become more goal oriented? Set personal goals; be tough
on yourself. Set organizational/church goals, follow through, and evaluate. And,
in the process, be accountable to someone. This factor will ensure that you
keep your commitments to your goals.

Although Spurgeon lived only to the age of fifty-seven, his far-reaching accomplishments shine forth as an example of what one can achieve when commitment and competence characterize one's life. He was willing to take the
gifts and abilities that he possessed and work hard so that he would become
more skilled in and better prepared for his service to the Lord. Any aspiring
Christian leader today who hopes to achieve much and have a lasting impact
will make a similar determination, offering his best to God and seeking to
develop the leadership capacity that God has given to him.

SPURGEON'S LEADERSHIP LESSONS

- **Competence in ministry is necessary for leaders to make progress in their service to Christ.** Spurgeon's commitment to training and education led him to found The Pastors' College, intended for the practical instruction of ministers who would be serving in local pastorates. The leader today must have a similar commitment to personal ministerial competence.
- **A leader committed to ministerial competence will continue to develop his leadership skills.** Although Spurgeon did not pursue formal theological training, he was self-taught and widely read, which enabled him to exercise better his spiritual gifts and grow in his leadership capacities.
- **Leaders must communicate to lead effectively.** Spurgeon gave several admonitions regarding communication, notably regarding preaching. He issued four directives: cultivate a clear style, cultivate a cogent style, cultivate naturalness, and cultivate persuasiveness.
- **A leader demonstrates competence by the ability to train and equip the people in their service to Christ.** Spurgeon said of Jesus, "He called disciples to Him one by one, and instructed each one with patient care." Spurgeon engaged in leadership training through The Pastors' College, the eldership at the Metropolitan Tabernacle, and other ministries.
- **A leader's influence is not so much position, but effectiveness in one's personal ministry.** Spurgeon wrote, "Ministers are servants; they are not guests, but waiters; not landlords, but labourers." Throughout his life, Spurgeon maintained his commitment to engage in personal ministry, setting aside specific times for interaction/counseling with his members.
- **Competence in leadership also depends on one's skills in relating to people.** Spurgeon said, "Look to the interests of all who are in Christ Jesus, and let them all be as dear to you as your own children. . . . Our Lord would have us thus identify ourselves with His holy business; and especially, He would have us love His chosen."
- **A leader must set goals to accomplish the tasks that God has called him to do.** Spurgeon's first goal was to glorify God through his ministry. An important part of that goal was his desire to reach people for Christ. He believed that evangelism and other ministry goals must be intentional if one is to achieve his aim in serving the Lord.

2

CONFIDENCE

Balancing Faith, Attitude, Initiative, and Humility

*It is essential that we should exhibit faith in the form
of* confidence in God.[1]

One of the greatest blessings for a leader is to know that he is in the center of
God's will for his life! Such assurance brings a confidence to one's leadership
and ministry that cannot be supplied by any other motivation.

Eric Liddell, the aspiring Olympic runner from Scotland, displayed such
confidence. In the Oscar-winning movie *Chariots of Fire*, a striking scene occurred in which Liddell was upbraided by his sister after arriving late at a gospel mission service that he was supposed to lead. He had been caught up in
training for the 1924 Olympics in Paris and had lost track of the hour. His
sister believed that his tardiness was an indication that he was putting his running ahead of God. Eric sought to assure his sister that he intended to follow
God's plan for his life, but part of that plan was for him to run in the Olympic
games. In a tense but tender moment, he grasped her shoulders, looked her
squarely in the eyes, and stated confidently, "Jenny, God made me for a purpose. But He also made me fast. And when I run, I feel His pleasure." Liddell
pursued his running goal enthusiastically and proceeded to win a gold medal
in the 1924 Olympics. He then kept his commitment to God and followed his
calling to serve as a missionary to China. There he remained until he was
martyred during the Communist occupation in the late 1940s.

Eric Liddell knew the joy and confidence that came from the surety and
certainty of his faith. In the same sense, Charles Spurgeon knew the spiritual

confidence that issued from his faith in God. Reflecting on his conversion, Spurgeon recalled the direct challenge from the lay minister who spoke the morning he came to personal faith in Christ. The speaker had looked straight at the teenage boy and exhorted him, "Young man, you look miserable . . . you must look to Jesus." Spurgeon later wrote: "By looking to Him, I received all the faith which inspired me with confidence in His grace; and the word that first drew my soul—"Look unto Me"—still rings its clarion note in my ears. There I once found conversion, and there I shall ever find refreshing and renewal.[2]

Throughout his remarkable ministry, Spurgeon had an innate confidence in the grace of God that overflowed like a bubbling brook from his life to others. He believed firmly that God had called him. He was convinced that God had a great plan for his life. He was assured that God would use him, and he lived with the resolve that he could accomplish all things through the power of the Lord! His determination stemmed not from any confidence in himself but rather an unabashed confidence in the goodness and greatness of God.

Confidence and Faith

Leaders typically display a measurable amount of confidence, but they must be careful that it is the right type of confidence. Those who trust in only themselves display incredible ignorance about the source of true power. They are the unfortunate ones who possess a misdirected and misplaced confidence—in their own ability.

All too often, we see this egotistical pattern in the moneygrubbing, dog-eat-dog corporate world. Aspiring power brokers trample on underlings who get in their way as they grope for recognition and achievement. We see self-aggrandizement in the political world. During elections, office seekers use negative campaigning and character assassination against their opponents in an attempt to show their superiority and secure victory. We see self-idolization in the athletic world. Superstars who experience a certain type of idol worship begin to believe the media hype about themselves and conduct themselves in a way that says, "The world is here to serve me!" We even see self-worshiping leaders in the church. They are people who lose sight of God's vision and aspire to build their own personal kingdoms on earth. All of these examples have one thing in common—an arrogant confidence that virtually omits God.

Spurgeon was leery of any confidence outside of Christ. He warned of godless self-confidence: "There is nothing more true than the fact that the self-confident are near a fall, that those who lean on themselves must be overthrown, and that carnal security has but a baseless fabric in which to dwell."[3] He believed that one could not be used of God until self-confidence was depleted:

> Our Heavenly Father does not usually cause us to seek the Savior till He has whipped us clean out of all our confidence; He cannot make us in earnest after Heaven till He has made us feel something of the intolerable tortures of an aching conscience, which is a fore-taste of hell.[4]

When Spurgeon saw his own sinful state, his own notions about personal confidence vanished. His oft-seared conscience forbade such fanciful notions. As he experienced personal conviction concerning his sinful condition, which led to his subsequent conversion, the young Spurgeon realized his need to place his confidence where it belonged—in God, through faith in Christ. He had remembered what he had learned from his studies in the Scriptures.

Faith in God's Power

Spurgeon recalled Paul's words: "Whether you eat or drink or whatever you do, do it all for the glory of God" (1 Cor. 10:31 NIV). When Spurgeon came to faith, he developed a profound passion to please God. It became his lifelong goal as he followed his calling, and subsequently when he became a spiritual leader, to do everything to bring glory to God. It was not just a convenient public relations tool. Bringing glory to God was Spurgeon's true motivation. His whole aim was to live for Him, that God would gain the glory from his earthly efforts. The Lord instilled in Spurgeon through his strong faith a rock-ribbed confidence that affected every area of his life and ministry. As he reflected later in life on his own experience, he compelled other pastors to follow suit: "It is essential that we should exhibit faith in the form of *confidence in God*."[5]

Spurgeon had confident faith—faith in God's power. It gave him strength to serve and to lead. Early in his ministry, at his first church in the village of Waterbeach, Spurgeon spoke on the theme "Jehovah-Jireh"—"I am ever with you." He declared his biblical points: "It is better to trust in the Lord than to put confidence in man. . . . It is better to trust in the Lord than to put confidence in princes. . . . Underneath thee are the everlasting arms. Never have I sought in vain."[6]

Spurgeon's confidence was an indelible faith in God. He continuously accessed that confidence. He was confident in God's authority, His rule, and His sovereignty. Spurgeon believed that God was in total control. Such confidence helped him to know his place in relation to God. Spurgeon was confident in knowing that Christ builds the church. He realized that every true church belongs to Him. He believed that the local church is important to God's plan. Spurgeon had confidence in the authority of God's Word. For him, it was the ultimate instruction book for life and ministry. These were the sources of power in his life.

Faith in God's Promises

Some Christian leaders battle a lack of confidence in their calling/ministry. Through the trials of their calling, they might have lost confidence in their spiritual leadership. Perhaps they have their eyes on themselves rather than on God.

How can one become more confident? It sounds simple but is profoundly true: have faith in God. Draw closer to Jesus. Believe the promises of His Word! Spurgeon wrote, "Brothers, if you do not believe in anybody else, believe in God without stint. Believe up to the hilt. Bury yourselves, both as to your weakness and strength, in simple trust in God."[7]

What is the result of such trust? It is a sense of assurance that God is with us, that He will not forsake us. Spurgeon understood the Source of his achievements. In one of his chapters in *An All-Round Ministry,* he referred to his contemporary, George Müller, the great founder of Christian orphanages in England. Müller was known to depend completely on God for all things. He never asked for any money and yet raised thousands of pounds through his childlike faith in God. Spurgeon remembered his friend's faith:

> Dependence upon God is the flowing fountain of success. That true saint of God, George Müller, has always struck me, when I have heard him speak, as being such a simple, child-like being in his dependence upon God; but, alas! Most of us are far too great for God to use us; we can preach as well as anybody, make a sermon with anybody—and so we fail. Take care, brethren, for if we think we can do anything of ourselves, all we shall get from God will be the opportunity to try.[8]

Spurgeon believed that many ministers missed their truest success because they trusted in themselves rather than in God. They could reverse that trend by trusting in God and claiming His promises for their lives.

Faith in God's Providence

Confident leaders are spiritually decisive. They are able to make responsible decisions. They have a built-in authority related to their calling and relationship with Christ. Spurgeon believed that all things are possible for a leader who trusts God each step of the way. Confidence increases when a small task is done well. A leader then can take on larger tasks as well. Spurgeon's opportunities increased as he exercised the confidence that God gave to him. It was a confidence that helped him through trying times.

On one significant occasion, Spurgeon's confidence in God was tested. As Spurgeon's church at New Park Street was being renovated, the congregation had to meet in a secular hall. The Royal Surrey Gardens Music Hall was secured for their evening services. On the morning of that first meeting, Spurgeon had preached on the theme "Prove Me Now," and he believed that some great trial was to come. His foreboding was confirmed when a tragic incident occurred that night in the Music Hall.

So many people came to hear Spurgeon that the place was filled to overflowing. Someone estimated that more than ten thousand people were in attendance. Early in the service, someone shouted, "Fire!" Spurgeon did not hear the person, but a great commotion occurred among the congregation. People started running for the doors. In the rush, seven people were trampled to death. Spurgeon, unaware of the problem at the back, continued the service. Afterward, when he learned what had happened, he was cut to the heart with horror. The press criticized him for allowing it to happen and continuing the service. He fell into a deep depression. Miraculously, he was back in his pulpit in only eight days, but the memories of that event troubled him for years to come.

Later, writing in his autobiography, Spurgeon shared the experience in third person:

> Amidst fightings without and fears within, he was enabled to proclaim the strongest confidence in God. He has made that proof, which he counseled others to make, of the Divine faithfulness; and

as to the result (notwithstanding a parenthesis of grievous tribulation), he dares to speak with abundant gratitude.[9]

It was Spurgeon's abiding trust in the providence of God that sustained him through a most perilous time.

Confidence and Attitude

The proper perspective is imperative for leaders to pursue their calling with confidence. The wrong perspective can result in dire consequences. As a leader looks at his own situation, he should ask, "Is the glass half empty or half full?" One's perspective in answering that question reveals much about the person's attitude.

One would think that most leaders would be positive in their outlook, especially if their faith is in Christ. Unfortunately, a lot of "stinkin' thinkin'," as someone has termed it, exists even among Christian leaders. The writer of Proverbs tells us, "As he thinketh in his heart, so is he" (23:7 KJV). If a person's attitude is negative, the result can become a self-fulfilling prophecy. People don't respond to negativity. They want to follow someone who is positive, hopeful, and full of faith in the Lord.

Real leadership issues from a state of mind, not from the tag of a certain status or position. Leaders might be tempted to think that their title or office brings its own commendation. John Maxwell, in his book *Developing the Leader Within,* writes, "Leadership has less to do with position than it does with disposition."[10] Attitude determines altitude. You will go as high as the aspirations that inspire you. Your attitude will affect the attitudes of your followers. They will be confident as you are confident. Again, it comes down to influence. To exert the right influence, a leader must be positive. So be a faith-filled and hope-filled person. Be optimistic. Be the most enthusiastic person you know. Be passionate. Be inspiring. Know your role and what you're dealing out to your followers. Napoleon believed that "a leader is a dealer in hope."[11]

Christians have every reason to be confident. Our future is sure and certain through Jesus Christ. "No eye has seen, no ear has heard, no mind has conceived what God has prepared for those who love him" (1 Cor. 2:9 NIV). We await His glorious return and our victorious consummation!

Spurgeon was certain of the ultimate outcome: "We, therefore, in confidence wait, and in patience bide our time. We are sure of victory ere long."[12]

Spurgeon's Persuasion

Shortly after Spurgeon began to preach in London at the New Park Street Baptist Church, the congregation grew so quickly that the building was not large enough to hold the worshipers. Finally, in his frustration at the lack of response by the deacons to do anything about it, Spurgeon preached a sermon on the battle of Jericho. In the midst of his message, he declared, "By faith, the walls of Jericho fell down; and by faith, this wall at the back shall come down, too."

After the service, an older deacon, in somewhat domineering tones, spoke to the young minister, and said, "Let us never hear of that again."

Spurgeon recalled, "'What do you mean?' I inquired; 'you will hear no more about it *when it is done,* and therefore the sooner you set about doing it, the better.'"[13]

Although not every pastor might get away with such a pronouncement, the increasing attendance supported Spurgeon's argument. Shortly thereafter, the church proceeded to make the necessary renovations to enlarge the building.

Followers reflect the attitude of their leaders. Spurgeon mourned the state of some dead churches that had dead leaders:

> I am very thankful that I have never been the pastor of a dead church, controlled by dead deacons. I have seen such a thing as that with my own eyes, and the sight was truly awful. I recollect very well preaching in a chapel where the church had become exceedingly low, and, somehow, the very building looked like a sepulcher, though crowded that one night by those who came to hear the preacher. The singers drawled out a dirge, while the members sat like mutes. I found it hard preaching; there was no go in the sermon, I seemed to be driving dead horses. After the service, I saw two men, who I supposed were the deacons,—the pillars of the church,—leaning against the posts of the vestry door in a listless attitude, and I said, "Are you the deacons of this church?" They informed me that they were the only deacons, and I remarked that I thought so. . . . Here was a dead church, comparable to the ship of the ancient mariner which was manned by the dead. Deacons, teachers, minister, people, all dead, and yet wearing the semblance of life.[14]

Christians serve a risen Savior! We have more reason than anyone to be purveyors and conveyors of life. A leader who is alive and enthusiastic and exhibits the right attitude will attract people who are looking for a living, vibrant Christian ministry with which they can become involved.

Perspective and Possibilities

Some leaders are hesitant to move forward and make important decisions because of their own dismal attitude. They demonstrate a lack of faith, and it affects their followers. Spurgeon wrote, "I make bold to assert that, in the service of God, nothing is impossible, and nothing is improbable. Go in great things, brethren, in the Name of God; risk everything on His promise, and according to your faith shall it be done unto you."[15]

Christian leader Chuck Swindoll reinforces Spurgeon's belief with his statement that life is 10 percent what happens to me and 90 percent how I react to it. Maxwell echoes that sentiment: "Positive thinking does not always change our circumstances, but it will always change us. When we are able to think right about tough situations, then our journeys through life become better."[16]

How can a leader have a better attitude? Practice being positive. It's easy to be negative. You can hear a hundred positive statements and then hear one negative comment. What happens? You remember the one negative statement. Develop a plan for right thinking. Associate with positive people who encourage you. Their spirit will become contagious. Read motivational works. Soak yourself in the Psalms and other inspiring Scriptures. Develop the habit of spending time reading motivational and encouraging devotional books. Set a goal of being positive about certain things each day. Count your blessings. Cultivate a pattern of positive achievement. The resulting positive attitude will pay dividends of blessing that you never imagined possible.

Confidence and Initiative

A leader who has confidence in God will take the initiative to direct and lead in his ministry. The leader becomes active, not passive, in his approach—proactive, not reactive, waiting for something to happen. It's important to be a self-starter.

Spurgeon saw great reluctance among many leaders: "The common policy of our churches is that of great prudence. We do not, as a rule, attempt anything beyond our strength. . . . We accomplish little because we have no idea of doing much. I would to God we had more 'pluck.'"[17]

Although *pluck* might be an outdated term, it connotes Spurgeon's notion of a determined resolve to move forward in the name of Christ. Most of us have heard the seven last words of a dying church: "We never did it that way before." The leader must ensure that those words are not used to describe the church that he, stepping out in faith, leads with confidence.

Self-Discipline

Initiative doesn't just happen; it takes great discipline in one's work habits. Many leaders become complacent. Complacency in one's accomplishments is something to be feared. You can get used to the norm, the routine, and the predictable. It might become quite comfortable. But is it where God intends for you to be? The preacher's task is to exhort his followers to venture forth out of their comfort zones: to comfort the afflicted and afflict the comfortable. The preacher, the leader, also needs to heed the message himself; he must be careful not to fall into the trap of comparing himself favorably with other leaders who are doing less. Spurgeon warned of the danger of such comparisons:

> Let us not judge ourselves by others, and say, with deadening self-complacency, "We are getting on well as compared with our brethren. There are not many additions to our churches, but we are as successful as others." O brother, if some are still further behind in the course, that does not increase our hope of winning the race! Let us measure ourselves by our Master, and not by our fellow-servants; then pride will be impossible, but hopefulness will be natural.[18]

The leader who takes initiative is a motivator. As people are motivated, they become inspired, and their morale is raised in the process. Peter Wagner shows the positive effects of good morale: (1) Morale builds through a contagious sense of expectancy. (2) Morale builds through a series of good experiences. (3) Morale builds through God-given achievement.[19] Congregations, businesses, and other organizations need leaders who will inspire, encourage, and motivate them toward higher goals.

Working Smart

The good leader knows when to take the initiative. He works hard and, more importantly, works smart. He knows what to do himself and what can be delegated to others. The successful leader is the one who makes the right move at the right moment with the right motive. Such leadership calls for diligence and perseverance. Spurgeon declared, "Be diligent in action. Put all your irons into the fire. Use every faculty for Jesus. Be wide-awake to watch opportunities, and quick to seize upon them."[20]

A leader with initiative is usually the same leader who strives for excellence. He doesn't settle for mediocrity and doesn't try to get by with the minimal amount of effort. He is the one who goes the extra mile, burns the midnight oil, and does more than is expected of him. Spurgeon became irritated when he saw gifted pastors frittering away their opportunities:

> Some of our brethren have held on under fearful discouragements, serving the Lord faithfully; others have won souls for Christ, to whom the winning of one soul has cost more self-denial than the winning of hundreds has cost certain of us. I could sit with delight at the feet of such consecrated brethren as I am now thinking of, and look up to them, and glorify God in them. Such have been found among men of inferior abilities, slender powers, and small attainments; but how they have worked, and how they have prayed, and how God has blessed them! It may be that, with ten times their ability and opportunity, we have not done anything like as much as they have. Do we not mourn over this? Can we afford to decline?[21]

Spurgeon believed that with giftedness and opportunity comes great responsibility. God will not look lightly upon a leader who pursues his calling passively.

As a leader, how can you be a better initiator? Take it upon yourself to pursue your work with a dogged determination and a consummate passion. Work as if everything depends on you; pray as if everything depends on God. Although we know that the Lord does not expect us to do anything in our own strength, He does expect us to pour ourselves into our work and ministry. Then, in the final analysis, we can leave the results with Him.

Confidence and Humility

The balance between confidence and humility enables a leader to exercise his gifts responsibly, looking to God but also having an appreciation of one's own abilities. Regardless of one's abilities or accomplishments, however, there is no place for arrogance. Arrogance is the result of pride and selfishness. A leader who experiences some measure of success is no doubt tempted toward boastfulness and self-exaltation. But anyone who sees himself as a servant of Christ will recognize the need for humility. Such humility is not false humility, which is self-deprecating and says, "I'm no good, I can't do anything." A person with true humility sees himself as Christ would see him.

When Spurgeon first went to London, rather than being overjoyed by his success, he was "appalled" by it:

> When I first became a Pastor in London, my success appalled me; and the thought of the career which it seemed to open up, so far from elating me, cast me into the lowest depth.... Who was I that I should continue to lead so great a multitude? I would betake me to my village obscurity, or emigrate to America, and find a solitary nest in the backwoods, where I might be sufficient for the things which would be demanded of me. It was just then that the curtain was rising upon my life-work, and I dreaded what it might reveal. I hope I was not faithless; but I was timorous, and filled with a sense of my own unfitness. I dreaded the work which a gracious Providence had prepared for me.[22]

Spurgeon knew what he was and where he came from. But he also recognized that he was a child of the King. Regardless of his own misgivings, he served a God who was able to accomplish much through him if he was willing to be used by Him. Spurgeon's forthright confidence rested in God's ability to accomplish His purposes through him and other leaders:

> All the purposes of man have been defeated, but not the purposes of God. The promises of man may be broken—many of them are made to be broken—but the promises of God shall all be fulfilled. He is a promise-maker, but He never was a promise-breaker; He is a promise-keeping God, and every one of His people shall prove it

to be so. This is my grateful, personal confidence, "The Lord will perfect that which concerneth me" unworthy me, lost and ruined me. He will yet save me; and *"I, among the blood-wash'd throng, Shall wave the palm, and wear the crown, and shout loud victory."*[23]

Egotism and Egoism

As his ministry flourished, Spurgeon was accused occasionally of being arrogant. He would counter that he was confident but only because of the Lord's presence in his life. He distinguished the difference between egotism and egoism thus:

> The proper recognition of the EGO is a theme worthy of our attention. I will make a word if I may: Let EGOTISM stand for proud, vainglorious, intrusive selfhood, and let EGOISM stand for the humble, responsible, and honest selfhood, which, finding itself in being, resolves to be at the Divine bidding, and to be at its best, to the glory of God.[24]

He was willing to grant that he had an ego, but he sought to let the Lord harness that ego for holy purposes.

Shining Christ's Light

Spurgeon lived out Jesus' teaching: "Let your light so shine before men, that they may . . . glorify your Father" (Matt. 5:16 KJV). He saw no need to hide his light under a bushel. But, he did seek to maintain a proper relationship of his ego with an unreserved submission to the lordship of Christ. Spurgeon believed, like John the Baptist, "He must increase, but I must decrease" (John 3:30 KJV). The greater his relationship to Christ, the more confident he became in the Lord's work. At the same time, he realized the need to reduce focus on himself.

Humility demonstrates a servant's heart. It shows a willingness to listen, to learn, and to admit when one is wrong. Spurgeon did not fear the confidence that is tempered by humility:

> There is a confidence in one's own powers which must ever be of

service to those who are called to eminent positions, provided the confidence is well-grounded, seasoned with humility, and attended with that holy gratitude which refers all honor and glory to the Giver of every good and perfect gift.[25]

Humility means that one always remains teachable. It means that one is willing to let others get the credit. Too often, Christian pastors are unwilling to involve others in ministry because they want to keep the credit for themselves. That is not servant leadership or true humility. Followers are impressed by leaders who are willing to share the success and glory along the way.

Believing the Best in Others

Spurgeon had plenty of reason to doubt the sincerity of his brethren in the ministry. Many of them were critical of him and jealous of his success. He knew the reality of the statement that many folks are quite willing to weep with you when you weep but not willing to rejoice with you when you rejoice. He determined to believe the best regarding the intentions of his fellow ministers. He said, "Learn to disbelieve those who have no faith in their brethren. Suspect those who would lead you to suspect others. A resolute unbelief in all the scandalmongers will do much to repress their mischievous energies."[26] His goal was to edify and support his brothers in the faith, believing that he identified with their struggles as well as their victories.

Secure in Service

Spurgeon's followers would have considered him a leader rather than a boss. The difference was in the way he shared his heart and life with them. Typically, a boss says, "Go!" But a leader says, "Let's go!" A person who thinks himself too important to serve alongside his followers is basically insecure.

During the year of the cholera epidemic in London, Spurgeon showed that he was willing to get alongside the ones who were contagious and near death. His concern for others and his risking his own health endeared him to his church. They knew that he was willing to serve among them.

The secure leader is confident in his ability to lead and to serve others in the process. Too often, leaders have adopted professional attitudes that create barriers between them and their followers. They have come to believe that they are to be served rather than to serve. Os Guiness, author of *Dining with the Devil*, writes about this type of leader in the local church: "Many super-churches are simply artificially inflated local churches with charismatically inflated super-pastors that will not be able to survive their supergrowth."[27]

The humble leader recognizes his weaknesses and strengths. Spurgeon witnessed, "It is admirable to see a man humbly conscious of his own weakness, and yet bravely confident in the Lord's power to work through his infirmity."[28]

How can a leader be more humble? Seek God's will first. Put others ahead of your own desires. Look for opportunities to serve. Don't be conceited because of position. Serve others through grace and love. A leader with supreme confidence in God demonstrates a unique blend of God-confidence and self-humility, positive in his perspective and willing to initiate and take the lead when given the opportunity.

SPURGEON'S LEADERSHIP LESSONS

- **The Christian leader has an innate confidence that springs from knowing that he/she is in the center of God's will.** Spurgeon recognized that infinite source of confidence at an early age and persistently pursued God's will.
- The best exercise of faith is one's complete trust and confidence in God. Spurgeon urged his readers, "It is essential that we should exhibit faith in the form of *confidence in God.*"
- **Leaders who trust in themselves display incredible ignorance about the source of true power.** Spurgeon believed that one could not be used of God until self-confidence was depleted: "Our Heavenly Father does not usually cause us to seek the Savior till He has whipped us clean out of all our confidence."
- **The proper attitude/perspective is imperative for leaders to pursue their calling with confidence.** The degree to which a leader embodies a positive attitude may go a long way in determining one's effectiveness.
- **A leader who has confidence in God is empowered to take self-initiative in his ministry.** "Be diligent in action. Put all your irons into the fire. Use every faculty for Jesus. Be wide-awake to watch opportunities, and quick to seize upon them."
- **Leaders should be careful not to compare themselves with other leaders.** "Let us not judge ourselves by others. . . . Let us measure ourselves by our Master, and not by our fellow-servants; then pride will be impossible, but hopefulness will be natural."
- **The balance between confidence and humility enables a leader to exercise his/her gifts responsibly.** "The proper recognition of the EGO is a theme worthy of our attention . . . the humble, responsible, and honest selfhood . . . resolves to be at the Divine bidding, and to be at its best, to the glory of God."
- **The humble leader recognizes his weaknesses and strengths.** "It is admirable to see a man humbly conscious of his own weakness, and yet bravely confident in the Lord's power to work through his infirmity."
- **Confidence, tempered by humility, seeks to bring all glory to God.** "There is a confidence in one's own powers which . . . is well-grounded, seasoned with humility, and attended with that holy gratitude which refers all honor and glory to the Giver of every good and perfect gift."

3

CONTEXT

Spurgeon in Victorian England

We have abundant reason to be thankful for the peace and order which we have enjoyed during the memorable reign of Queen Victoria. God grant that we may not have to learn the value of our blessings by the loss of them![1]

"The history of a country, or its religion, cannot be studied in isolation."[2] What is true of the history of a nation is true also in the study of a person. A leader cannot be separated from the background, environment, culture, and multiple influences that contribute to his development as a person. Every leader is as much a product of the composite of forces and factors that helped to shape and inform his life as he is an influence on the lives of others.

It is imperative to place a study of C. H. Spurgeon's leadership in the context of nineteenth-century Victorian England. To grasp better the significance of his leadership and its impact on the people of his day, one must view Spurgeon as a man of his times. The aim of this chapter is to gain a greater understanding of Spurgeon and his unique contribution to Christian leadership by painting a broad picture of the sociological and religious forces that formed the backdrop of his ministry.

The Cultural Context

One historian stated that it is not correct to stereotype the Victorian Age as "a succession of mere storms in a teacup. It was rather a period of explosions— of political, social, moral, scientific and religious revolution."[3] This quotation seems to be an apt description of nineteenth-century England. Great Britain

was changing rapidly in the 1800s, and the process of social upheaval throughout the nation was affecting many of its citizens.

Charles Haddon Spurgeon was born in 1834, three years before Queen
Victoria ascended the English throne. He entered the world in rural Essex
county amid relative calm. Elsewhere, in more urban settings, the nation was
reeling from the swift social changes that were taking place. Significant national reforms were on the rise. The Parliamentary Reform Bill of 1832 was
enacted to give voting rights to low-income citizens for the first time. Slavery
was abolished in 1833, and laws were passed fixing the working hours of children in factories.

The Stability of Queen Victoria

A young Victoria assumed the throne as queen of England at the age of
eighteen. She reigned until her death in 1901, a span of sixty-four years. Her
accession in the country's royal leadership marked the utter transformation of
the crown and court. Victoria returned respectability and moral accountability to the throne, in stark contrast to the previous disreputable monarchy of
the decadent William IV. She exercised decisive leadership and a strong moral
influence that was felt in both government and daily life. Her stability on the
throne allowed Britain to extend its empire greatly, and the economy of the
nation grew considerably. Although the Puritan ruler Oliver Cromwell was
one of Spurgeon's heroes, he was a royalist at heart. He greatly admired Queen
Victoria and was very loyal to her sovereign rule over the British Empire.

The Victorian era was the triumph of industrialization, as Britain paved the
way for the rest of the world. The erection of factories filled with textile ma-
chinery, the domination of locomotives and steamships in travel, and the re-
placement of candles and lamps with gas lighting signaled the eventual decline
of an agricultural society and the rise of a mechanized society. A host of goods
produced in Britain flooded the British Empire as exports increased dramatically. They were accompanied by new classes of industrialists and tradesmen,
all part of the developing secular society.

Urban Poverty

The advance of the British economy, however, did not affect all of the populace positively. Productivity was based on the mass labor of the poor, includ-

ing women and children, in appalling work conditions. Remuneration for the long days of hard labor was small. Trade unions were in the early stages of organization, but poverty among the lower wage earners was excessive. The smoke, grease, and grime from the factories covered the beautiful buildings of London and filled the city with its infamous yellow fogs. The slum dwellers lived among filth and disease as London's population mushroomed from one to two million during the course of the nineteenth century.

Some of the socially conscious members of the growing middle class gradually became aware that something had to be done to change the oppressive conditions of the nation's poor. Shopkeepers, public-house proprietors, and others in the working class agreed with some members of the privileged upper class who came to believe that society should protect those who would suffer most from the emerging social and economic forces. Thus, they became involved to reform prisons, repeal cruel labor laws, fight child labor, and generally endorse the propagation of education and philanthropy. Out of this effort came the response of C. H. Spurgeon and various other religious leaders to advance forms of individual philanthropy. Their belief was that in helping individuals, society would benefit as a result. Thus, they instituted orphanages, almshouses, and other ministries to meet the social ills of their time.

The Cholera Epidemic

In 1854, the first year that Spurgeon lived and ministered in London, the great cholera epidemic raged across the city. He was required continuously to attend the bedside of dying victims or the gravesides of those who had succumbed. He noticed that some of his pastoral friends were contracting the disease, and it worried him. One day, after returning home from a funeral, Spurgeon noticed a paper that was stuck in a shoemaker's window. As he pulled it out, and unfolded it, he took to heart the words thereon: "Because thou has made the Lord, which is my refuge, even the Most High, thy habitation; there shall no evil befall thee, neither shall any plague come nigh thy dwelling." From that time on, Spurgeon continued to minister to the sick and dying, in confidence that he would remain well, and he was blessed to do so at that time.

This social climate was the environment in which C. H. Spurgeon and others ministered in the middle Victorian years. Poverty, disease, and moral degradation were rampant among the squalid masses of urban areas such as East London. These conditions aroused the consciences of many Christians, and new ideas evolved; thus, philanthropic movements were set in motion to meet the needs of the poor. Spurgeon, like other evangelicals of his day, did not see the dichotomy between the social aspects and the evangelistic aspects of the gospel. To him, it was not either/or but both/and regarding God's command to minister to body and soul. Through his leadership in ministerial endeavors, Spurgeon was able to wed the two aspects in a way that was biblically sound and morally advantageous to spreading the gospel.

The Religious Context

The changes occurring in other realms of society were bound to have ramifications for the religious realm. As English life generally was transformed through the revolution that occurred in the social and economic structures, the church was also affected. Victorian Christianity had to deal with the spiritual problems created by the new populations in the great towns, the growing separation of the classes, and the resultant difficulties that came from the rise of economic materialism.

In the midst of radical change in the country, organized religion seemed to be a critical force for stability. It provided assurance for a nation whose own progress and development helped to change the face of the world. But, religious expression was not static because its variety reflected the diversity of the times. Worship that occurred at the liturgical services held by the archbishop at Canterbury bore little resemblance to the gospel meetings held in a small Baptist chapel in Essex. The different styles of worship were symbolic of the complex religious matrix that characterized the Victorian era.

The Church of England

The dominant denomination of England by and large was the Established Church, the Church of England (commonly referred to as Anglican). It was supported by the government and was granted privileges that others outside its parishes did not enjoy. Before the laws were changed through reforms in the early 1800s, only members of the Church of England could participate in parliament, municipal corporations, the bench, or the bar and attend universities.

Spurgeon's family came from a long line of Puritan Dissenters (grouped among the Nonconformists), members of denominations that were outside the Established Church. As the nineteenth century progressed, restrictions against the non-Anglican denominations were relaxed, and the Dissenting churches came to enjoy more political and religious freedom as time passed. As they exercised their new-found freedoms, they became more powerful, and their influence was felt in the political reforms of the day. The rise of Nonconformity with the ascent of denominations such as Baptist, Methodist, and Congregationalist created a more pluralistic religious scene. They rallied for constitutional reforms in England because the reforms made their position stronger in relation to the Established Church. Thus, the change in society effected changes in the religious realm and set the stage for developments that would alter the form of Christianity in England.

The Rise of Evangelicalism

Evangelical pietism was a powerful reaction to formal orthodoxy and rationalism that prevailed in the 1700s. The evangelicals sought to reach individuals with the gospel of Jesus Christ, believing that personal faith in Christ was essential for salvation. They revived personal Bible reading and individual commitment; modified intellectualism with emotional warmth; generated social concern; and rejuvenated preaching, missions, and hymnody. Although evangelicalism had an important influence in the Church of England, its fervor was greatest among the Dissenting churches. They grew tremendously in the 1800s as a result of the revival under George Whitefield and John Wesley during the preceding century.

By the middle of the nineteenth century, the number of active Nonconformists surpassed the number of practicing Anglicans. The largest non-Anglican denomination was Methodist, followed by Baptist. As these groups experienced growth, they produced preachers of great power. Indeed, one writer stated, "The number of Nonconformist preachers of merit was so considerable that it is exceedingly difficult to select names from among them for mention."[4] A few of them, however, were C. H. Spurgeon, Joseph Parker, Alexander Maclaren, and John Clifford, all of whom exemplified the increasing strength of the Dissenting pulpits.

The Missionary Movement

One of the most significant developments that arose from Nonconformity was the missionary movement of the nineteenth century. This period has been referred to as the "Great Century" of Protestant missionary outreach.[5] The vision for foreign missions that emerged in the person of William Carey was extended through the formation of many mission societies. They, in turn, sent hundreds of missionaries to all parts of the world in an effort to communicate the gospel to all peoples throughout the earth.

The growth of Nonconformist bodies did not occur without controversy. Historian Elliott-Binns referred to the "Dissidence of Dissent" that occurred with the multiplicity of Protestant groups.[6] The rising debate between the Established Church and the Dissenters, plus the competition between Dissenting denominations, meant numerous tensions in the religious world. Even within denominations arose conflicts that caused schisms and the formation of even more new religious groups. These struggles were part of the change that characterized Dissenting denominations during the Victorian era.

The Baptists

Shortly after his conversion, Spurgeon became a Baptist. Two main Baptist groups existed: the General Baptists, who held to Arminian doctrines, and the Particular Baptists, who were noted for their Calvinistic beliefs. Spurgeon was a Particular Baptist, holding to the beliefs that were typical of English Puritans and Separatists. During the 1800s, the General Baptists and the Particular Baptists maintained their distinctives but united for purposes of missions, evangelism, and fellowship. They formed what came to be known as the Baptist Union of Great Britain and Ireland. Spurgeon participated actively in the Baptist Union until his withdrawal toward the end of his ministry. His exit from the Baptist denomination will be addressed in a later chapter.

One event that had a great impact on religious change in Victorian England was the publication of Charles Darwin's *The Origin of Species* in 1859. Darwin's theories about evolution challenged orthodox Christian thinking. They also cast doubts on the supernatural involvement of God in the world. These doubts opened the way for acceptance of more liberal approaches to theology, which Spurgeon opposed throughout his ministry.

The general conditions of society and the needs of his day help us to understand why Spurgeon was able to gain widespread recognition. When he came to London, the masses of people were there, needing the influence of the gospel of Christ. The vast numbers in South London were ripe for evangelizing. With his exceptional preaching and multiple gifts of leadership, Spurgeon appeared on the scene at the right time and the right place to make a tremendous impact for the kingdom of God.

The Social Context

Spurgeon's unique contribution cannot be completely understood unless one keeps in mind the social picture of the time. Already, the great majority of the middle-class population attended church regularly each week. Normally, very few other distractions existed on Sunday. The Sunday excursion had not been thought of, and weekend trips had not become a habit. The very poor remained in their dwellings on Sundays, or they patronized the saloons or roamed the streets. Theaters were closed, and the era of the cinema had not yet arrived. There was nowhere else to attend on Sundays, at least for respectable people. There might have been a few exceptions, people who indulged in non-Sabbath revelries, but there was no open flaunting of such practices. The respectable middle classes went to church on Sunday morning, dined at midday, slept through the afternoon, and went to church again at night. Morning services were as largely attended as those of the evening, which were the more evangelistic of the two services. In those days, whole families worshiped together, and the family pew was a recognized institution.

Conventional Worship

The nature and description of churches in that day is also noteworthy. Most of them were bound by convention and tradition. Services, sermons, prayers, and hymns were lengthy—far too lengthy by contemporary expectations. The habit of ministers was to read their sermons, and many of them seemed to be extensive treatises, rather lifeless and boring. Preaching generally was methodical, predictable, intellectually weighty, and dull. Popular magazines ridiculed the typical clergymen in cartoons that portrayed them as aloof and out of touch. The advent of an aggressive, interesting person such as Spurgeon inspired other preachers to make church services more lively and their presentation more attractive.

Into the comparatively gray world of his London contemporaries, Spurgeon burst like a breath of fresh air. He began to reach common laborers and working-class persons with the saving message of the gospel. Before long, all types of people from different backgrounds were flocking to hear the young preacher from Essex. Eminent American pastor George W. Truett, speaking in 1934 at the centenary celebration of Spurgeon's birth at the Royal Albert Hall in London, remarked:

> He was a man of universal sympathies. Especially did his sympa-
> thies wholeheartedly go out to the poor, the needy, the ignorant,
> the unfortunate. The coming to his Tabernacle of Mr. Ruskin the
> scholar, or of Mr. Gladstone, the Prime Minister, or of Lord
> Shaftesbury, or of some far-famed Archbishop, gave him no more
> pleasure than the coming of the humble carpenter, the cabman, the
> seamstress, the washer-woman. In such fact, we have one of the
> most revealing explanations of his far-reaching influence and power.
> It could be said of him as of his Master: "The common people heard
> him gladly." With Paul he could say, and did say, "We then that are
> strong ought to bear the infirmities of the weak, and not to please
> ourselves." To him, the crowning glory of Christ's gospel is that it is
> to be preached to the poor.[7]

The Advent of Spurgeon

Many of his detractors prophesied that Spurgeon would not last, but they were mistaken. His effective ministry continued in London until the last year of his life, earning the respect of many of his peers and different leaders from all spheres of society. Not only did he influence London and much of England but also his published sermons and writings had a tremendous impact around the world. But it is essential to view Spurgeon as a leader in the context of his culture and society. Evidence suggests that he was as much a product of the forces of the times as he was an influence upon them. Indeed, all of the changes, reforms, growth, expansion, new ideas, and other terms used to describe Victorian England were part of the life experiences that shaped Spurgeon. Thus, given the sociocultural milieu in which he served, we are able better to understand the composite of his leadership.

Many changes have occurred since the Victorian era in which Spurgeon lived. In the opening years of a new millennium, as we face the challenges of Christian leadership in a highly technologically advanced society, many characteristics of his day seem remote and irrelevant. Yet, even with all of the social and cultural changes that have occurred during the last century, Spurgeon's spiritual leadership remains a popular and consistently high standard among evangelicals today. Many of the leadership principles that he personified are timeless because their basis was directly related to Spurgeon's understanding of the Word of God as applied to his life and ministry.

SPURGEON'S LEADERSHIP LESSONS

- **To understand a leader's influence, one must evaluate him in the context of his ministry.** Although Spurgeon was very successful in his day and time, one must set him and all other leaders within their context to understand their specific impact.
- **A leader cannot be separated from the background, environment, culture, and other multiple outside influences that contribute to his development as a person.** Every leader is as much a product of the composite of forces and factors that helped to shape and inform his life as he is an influence on the lives of others.
- **The social, economic, and cultural aspects of a society influence the extent of a leader's success.** Spurgeon described himself as a "capital man," a product of the scene in metropolitan London in the midst of a most conservative Victorian society. At the same time, his position of privilege stirred him to meet the needs of those less fortunate than himself.
- **A leader's vision is expanded through exposure to all of the needs of his surrounding environment.** When Spurgeon first entered the London scene, his encounter with the cholera epidemic provided the urgency for his evangelistic ministry. He did not shudder from his responsibility but shouldered more than his share in risking his own personal health to minister to the sick and dying.
- **The general state of society and the material conditions of the time help us to understand to some extent why Spurgeon attracted such widespread attention.** His style and approach to ministry were unique for his time because many of his peers were more reserved and predictable in their office. Spurgeon's aggressive approach to evangelism and ministry provided a platform for his widening influence.
- **A leader helps society by helping individuals.** Spurgeon and various other religious leaders sought to advance forms of individual philanthropy. Their belief was that society would benefit as a result of their helping individuals. Therefore, they instituted orphanages, almshouses, and other ministries to meet the social ills of their time.
- **Many spiritual leadership principles are timeless, regardless of social and cultural context.** The enduring standard of Spurgeon's leadership continues to this day because its basis was directly related to Spurgeon's understanding of the Word of God as applied to his life and ministry.

4

CALLING

Conversion and Growth

Brethren, you are not meant for anything but God; therefore,
surrender yourselves to God, and find in Him your wealth,
your honour, and your all.[1]

Charles H. Spurgeon was generally regarded as a godly man. His spiritual leadership ranked high among his peers and throughout Christendom in the nineteenth century. What was the secret of his holiness and his life of impeccable commitment to serving God? To answer that question, one must look to the source of Spurgeon's leadership, his life of faith based on his personal relationship to Jesus Christ. From that foundation came the spiritual resources that flowed continuously through his life to make him one of the most outstanding Christian leaders of his day.

One of the first principles to learn from the leadership of Charles Spurgeon is that a Christian leader must first be led by God before he can lead others. Assuredly, Spurgeon would have said "amen" to the scriptural admonition of Jesus to "seek first the kingdom of God and his righteousness" as the primary goal in one's spiritual commitment. Spurgeon's own experience of conversion and calling are instructive regarding the priority of spiritual commitment as the source of his leadership.

Spiritual Conversion

Charles Haddon Spurgeon was reared in a Christian home, both his father and his grandfather having served as ministers of the gospel. Children today who are fortunate enough to be born into and nurtured in evangelical Christian families often make early decisions for Christ, many before the age of ten. Spurgeon, although having received much spiritual instruction and training as a young boy, did not make his commitment to Christ until the age of fifteen. But the Christian influence of his family left an indelible impression upon him. Spurgeon later wrote of his spiritual training at home, "I was privileged with godly parents, watched over with jealous eyes, scarcely ever permitted to mingle with questionable associates, warned not to listen to anything profane or licentious, and taught the way of God from my youth up."[2]

The incidence of Spurgeon's conversion is oft recounted in the many biographies written about him. He often shared from the pulpit, especially in the latter years at the Metropolitan Tabernacle, his own experience of salvation. He was heard to say that an ounce of personal testimony was worth more than a ton of heavy theology. If he were struggling for something to say, he just put a charge of spiritual experience into the barrel and fired it off. Although he had plenty of spiritual ammunition from which to draw, his own conversion was near and dear to him throughout his life and ministry.

The Path to Salvation

Spurgeon could not be accused of "easy believism," the charge that is made today against a certain type of evangelism that asks for only intellectual assent to certain spiritual truths but does not call for personal repentance of one's sin and life-changing faith in Christ. Over a period of time, young Charles struggled with his own sinful condition and the need for personal spiritual conversion. He was well aware of the havoc of sin: "When I was in the hand of the Holy Spirit, under conviction of sin, I had a clear and sharp sense of the justice of God. Sin, whatever it might be to other people, became to me an intolerable burden. It was not so much that I feared hell, as that I feared sin."[3]

As a boy, Charles would regularly accompany his father as he preached in various Congregationalist churches. On one particularly cold, winter morning, the snow was so deep and the journey was so difficult that the young Spurgeon did not travel with his father. Instead, he sought the closest house of worship near his home. In the city of Colchester, on that wintry Sunday in January 1850, Spurgeon found a small Primitive Methodist church, where he stopped for worship. A guest speaker was featured that morning, a layman with little educational training who preached a simple gospel message based on Isaiah 45:22: "Look unto me, and be ye saved, all the ends of the earth"

(KJV). At one point, as the story goes, the layman looked out at Spurgeon and said, "Young man, you look very miserable."

The man's observation was correct; young Spurgeon stated that he felt most miserable indeed. The words struck right to his heart. The speaker continued, "You will always be miserable—miserable in life, and miserable in death—if you don't obey my text; but if you obey now, this moment, you will be saved. . . . Young man, look to Jesus Christ. Look! Look! Look! You have nothin' to do but look and live."[4] Immediately, Charles saw the way of salvation. He described it later: "There and then the cloud was gone, the darkness had rolled away, and that moment I saw the sun; and I could have risen that instant and sung with the most enthusiastic of them, of the precious blood of Christ, and the simple faith which looks alone to Him."[5] Spurgeon responded in faith, experienced forgiveness of his sin, and was truly converted to following Christ.

Believer's Baptism by Immersion

While his family had been Congregationalists who practiced infant baptism, young Charles had searched the Scriptures and came to a different conclusion on baptism. He was convinced that the Bible taught baptism as an ordinance to be practiced by full immersion and was for believers only. So he sought out a Baptist minister and discovered one in a village nearby. He immediately submitted to believer's baptism in obedience to Christ. Charles's willingness to act on conviction rather than his family's beliefs was indicative of the independent spirit with which he always approached matters of faith. If he was convinced that something was correct according to the Scriptures, Spurgeon was willing to stand alone against those who differed with him. This courageous spirit became a defining factor in leadership as Spurgeon later dealt with difficult issues of Christian faith and practice.

Spurgeon's father wrote, warning him that he should not trust in his baptism. The new convert assured his father that he held no superstitions that baptism would save him. His mother reminded him that although she had prayed often for his conversion, she had never prayed that he would become a Baptist. With humor, Charles responded "that the Lord had dealt with her in his usual bounty, and had given her exceedingly abundantly above what she had asked."[6]

On the day that Spurgeon was baptized, he was not the beneficiary of a warm, indoor, twenty-first-century baptistery. Rather, Spurgeon walked eight

miles to and from the site of his baptism, the small river Lark in a rural area of
Essex. It happened to be his mother's fiftieth birthday, and young Charles was
exhilarated to follow Christ's command to be baptized on such a memorable
occasion. Immediately thereafter, he became involved in Christian service, doing
anything he could to help others know the Christ whom he had come to know
as Lord and Savior.

Spurgeon's spiritual conversion was so profound that it became the primary motivation of his life as a Christian leader. From that time, his commitment was to witness to the salvation he experienced that others might be
brought to saving faith in Jesus Christ.

One would think that spiritual commitment would be a "given" for all Christian leaders. But Spurgeon later lamented the spiritual condition of some of
the so-called ministerial leaders of his day:

> I have heard of ministers who are most lively when playing croquet
> or cricket, or getting up an excursion, or making a bargain. It was
> said of one, in my hearing, "What a fine minister he would have
> been if he only had been converted." I heard it said of a very clever
> man, "He would have been a great winner of souls, if he had only
> believed in souls; but he believed in nothing."[7]

Spurgeon knew that it is imperative for Christian leaders first to know that
they are themselves transformed believers in Jesus Christ before they can expect to lead others to make a spiritual commitment of their own.

Vocational Calling

Kingdom leaders have a special calling to leadership. Paul wrote, "I thank
Christ Jesus our Lord, who hath enabled me, for that he counted me faithful,
putting me into the ministry" (1 Tim. 1:12 KJV). Whereas some contemporary
leaders refer to a "drivenness" in their lives, genuine Christian leaders function
from a true sense of calling. Jesus said, "Many are called, but few are chosen"
(Matt. 22:14 KJV). Those who respond to God's call find an identity, a security
that comes from knowing that they are in the center of God's will for their
lives. Spurgeon received a clarion call to ministry that sustained him throughout his illustrious career.

The Initial Call to Ministry

Many ministers have testified that their experience of receiving a vocational calling from God was one that they strongly resisted. They testify to a process that involved much struggle to "surrender" to that call in their lives. For Spurgeon, the call seemed less "surrender" than a more joyful acknowledgement of God's hand upon him. His calling seemed to develop as a natural progression of his passionate desire to serve the Christ who had saved him. As a young teenage Christian, he pursued actively opportunities to witness for Christ and accepted invitations to serve when they came. He began by teaching a boy's Sunday school class and then began receiving invitations to speak in different churches. It soon became apparent that God's anointing was upon the young lad from Essex. At the age of sixteen, the call to his first pastorate came from a thatched Baptist chapel in the village of Waterbeach. Just a little more than a year after his conversion, after the congregation had heard him speak only twice, they invited Spurgeon to become the church's leader. Charles felt the call as a confirmation of God's anointing to preach the gospel and accepted the church's invitation.

From the time he began preaching, Spurgeon's concern was the winning of souls to Christ. He knew that the gospel had saved him, but he wondered if it would save anyone else now that he preached it. After he had delivered his sermons the first couple of Sundays, he asked his deacons if anyone had been "brought to Christ" through his preaching. They responded that surely it must have happened, but Charles wanted to know for certain.

The day soon came when he heard about his first convert. One of his deacons told him, "It is a poor labourer's wife over at such-and-such a place! She went home broken-hearted by your sermon two or three Sundays ago, and she has been in great trouble of soul, but she has found peace, and she says she would like to speak to you."[8] Spurgeon went to visit her and reported that the reality of her conversion was like a seal upon his ministry.

Leading Others to Christ

A deep evangelistic commitment characterized Spurgeon's ministry from the outset. He counted the conversion of a person more precious than anything else:

> I would rather be the means of saving a soul from death than be the greatest orator on earth. I would rather bring the poorest woman in the world to the feet of Jesus than I would be made Archbishop of Canterbury. I would sooner pluck one single brand from the burning than explain all mysteries. To win a soul from going down into the pit, is a more glorious achievement than to be crowned in the arena of theological controversy as Dr. Sufficientissimus.[9]

The result of Spurgeon's evangelistic preaching was an overflowing church where many lives were transformed, in turn causing a profound effect upon the village. By the time Spurgeon was nineteen, word of his preaching ability had spread throughout the area. It was not long before the demand of his services came from various quarters.

The Call to London

A church in London that had once been the setting for outstanding ministry was searching for a pastor who might restore the church's former prominence. Park Street Baptist Church had been known for three notable pastors who had served there during their two hundred years of ministry: Benjamin Keach, Dr. John Gill, and Dr. John Rippon. Together, they contributed 148 years of significant ministry that enabled the church to grow and prosper. The church relocated and became New Park Street Baptist Church in the south part of London. Unfortunately, they settled in an area of the city that became depressed and uninhabited. This move, combined with the undistinguished ministries of four successive pastors, contributed toward the twelve hundred-capacity congregation's dwindling to only two hundred worshipers.

In the summer of 1853, they heard about the young pastor at Waterbeach and invited him to come and speak to the congregation. Spurgeon thought that a mistake had been made, thinking that they would not be interested in a country lad such as himself. But the church was most keen to secure his services, and when he preached to the church, the people were moved profoundly by the sermon. Word spread quickly, and the invitation came for Spurgeon to come to serve the historic congregation in the city of London. The advent of Spurgeon's ministry in London inaugurated an evangelistic pastorate that continued powerfully for close to thirty-eight years.

The Surety of the Calling

Throughout his ministry, Charles Spurgeon was overwhelmingly convinced of God's call on his life to vocational ministry. But he believed the call was connected directly to his spiritual commitment and obedience to Christ. Indeed, Spurgeon wrote that "true and genuine piety is necessary as the first indispensable requisite; whatever 'call' a man may pretend to have, if he has not been called to holiness, he certainly has not been called to the ministry."[10] Spurgeon sought continuous consecration to Christ, with the belief that the level of his own commitment validated his calling to serve and lead others.

Spurgeon was convinced that the basis of a leader's own faith commitment determines his effectiveness in ministry.

> Personal godliness must never grow scanty with us. Our own personal justification in the righteousness of Christ, our personal sanctification by the indwelling power of the Holy Spirit, our vital union with Christ, and expectancy of glory in Him, yea, our own advancement in grace, or our own declension; all these we must well know and consider.[11]

He believed that Christian ministers are to give themselves wholly to God:

> It needs no hesitation, the choice of every man among us is to be wholly the Lord's—ardently, passionately, vehemently the Lord's servants, let the Divine fervour cost us what it may of brain, and heart, and life. Our only hope of honour, and glory, and immortality lies in the fulfillment of our dedication unto God.[12]

Spurgeon believed that nothing is more important than a leader's calling: "Let each man find out what God wants him to do, and then let him do it, or die in the attempt."[13] Perhaps one reason why so many have left vocational ministry today is because their calling was not definitive. The Christian leader should be challenged by Spurgeon's unequivocal call to the ministry.

Determining One's Calling

How does one know whether he is called? As Spurgeon lectured to his students at The Pastors' College, he stated the following definitive signs for determining one's call to ministry.

1. *An intense, all-absorbing desire for the work.* There is an overwhelming passion for the ministry that motivates the leader to pursue it.
2. *Aptness to teach and some measure of the other qualities needful for a public instructor.* "A man must not consider that he is called to preach until he has proved that he can speak."[14]
3. *He must see a measure of conversion-work going on under his efforts.* Specifically related to the role of pastor, one must see evidence that one's ministry is resulting in the bringing of unsaved persons to Christ.
4. *His preaching should be acceptable to the people of God.* The people will provide sufficient testimony as to his "gifts, knowledge, and utterance."[15]

Spurgeon urged his students to be certain about their calling: "make sure work of it while you are yet in this retreat; and diligently labour to fit yourselves for your high calling."[16]

Spurgeon lamented the notion that ministers were serving in churches because it was their last vocational resort. "I have met ten, twenty, a hundred brethren, who have pleaded that they were sure, quite sure that they were called to the ministry—they were quite certain of it, because they had failed in everything else."[17] He believed that the call to serve God in a vocational capacity was the highest calling and the noblest of occupations. "On the whole, experience is our surest test, and if God upholds us from year to year, and gives us his blessing, we need make no other trial of our vocation."[18]

Perseverance in One's Calling

The rate at which ministers leave churches today is alarming. Many of them have been driven out because of moral failings and other improprieties. Some of them have experienced forced termination in ministry because of unmet expectations among the congregation. Also, a number of pastors have succumbed to "burnout," and find the stress of the ministry unbearable. Still others depart ministry for the promise of greener financial pastures in other professions. Spurgeon decried those who leave the ministry for other pursuits: "For us to turn aside from our life-work, and to seek distinction elsewhere, is absolute folly; a blight will be upon us, we shall not succeed in anything but the pursuit of God's glory."[19]

Spurgeon was convinced of the merit of long-term ministry: "It will be a sweet thing to have died at your post, not turning aside for wealth, or running from Dan to Beersheba to obtain a better salary, but stopping where your Lord bade you hold the fort."[20] He would be most chagrined by the short tenure of many ministers today, with averages estimated between two to three years per pastorate. It is little wonder that kingdom growth suffers when the evidence suggests pastors' tentative commitment to long-term ministry.

Did Spurgeon believe in running from trouble? Absolutely not. "Do not be afraid of hard work for Christ; a terrible reckoning awaits those who have an easy time in the ministry, but a great reward is in reserve for those who endure all things for the elect's sake."[21] He believed strongly in a lifetime commitment to vocational ministry based on one's sure and certain calling and a sacred determination to see it through to the end.

Commitment to Personal Spiritual Growth

The urgency of the times in which we live demands that one be committed to personal renewal and spiritual growth as a leader. The temptation is to become complacent and measure one's effectiveness by what other colleagues have done and are doing in their ministries. Spurgeon's response: "Let us measure ourselves by our Master, and not by our fellow-servants: then pride would be impossible, but hopefulness will be natural."[22] The Christian leader must be not only capable of growth that leads to greater opportunities but also resolved to continue in his spiritual development.

A leader will not lead others farther than he has gone himself. Perhaps this is why we see so many spiritually stagnated churches. Spurgeon said that it is most "important to the minister that his piety be vigorous. He is not to be content with being equal to the rank and file of Christians, he must be a mature and advanced believer; for the ministry of Christ has been truly called 'the choicest of his choice, the elect of his election, a church picked out of the church.'"[23] We would not want to be mentored by those who are no better than we ourselves. The same is true for those who follow our leadership. Spurgeon said, "I want a man who is better than myself to be my spiritual guide."[24]

A Resolve to Grow

Some leaders have the skills and the charisma, but they lack the resolve for increased spiritual development and make no commitment to long-term growth. Lacking the real resources that come from personal spiritual growth can prove lethal for those leaders who desire to extend their ministry. "Let this be the burning passion of your souls. *Grow to be leaders and champions.*"[25] Spiritual stagnation in a minister results in spiritual lethargy in the local church.

No reason exists for any spiritual leader to be satisfied with the status quo. Spurgeon wrote, "If we are to pursue our holy calling with success, *we need to be better men.*"[26] One may become contented having achieved certain goals and having reached a level of leadership success. But no reason ever exists for one to rest on one's laurels. Being a disciple means becoming a learner for life. The leader with a learning attitude who continues to grow spiritually will consolidate and expand his leadership effectiveness. One can never assume that one has arrived and has no need for further growth or spiritual development. Spurgeon wrote, "The most needful and profitable labour is that which we spend upon our own mental and spiritual improvement."[27] He saw the foolishness of the leader who continued to serve out of his own spiritual reserves but did not replenish his own spiritual energies: "To be always giving out, and never taking in, tendeth to emptiness."[28]

Prayer Empowered

What are some qualities that demonstrate spiritual growth? First, a leader must be prayer empowered. The Bible tells us to pray without ceasing. Spurgeon believed greatly in the need for prayer: "Make the most of prayer. . . . Prayer is the master-weapon. We should be greatly wise if we use it more, and did so with a more specific purpose."[29] Spurgeon was said never to have prayed more than five minutes at a time, but he never went more than five minutes without praying. He often mentioned that the secret of his success was prayer, and he cited the many church members who prayed regularly in the basement during the services and on other significant occasions.

Well-known church growth author/leader Peter Wagner writes, "The more deeply I dig beneath the surface of church growth principles, the more thoroughly convinced I become that the real battle is a spiritual battle and that our principle weapon is prayer."[30] An effective leader must have a deep prayer life. Spurgeon wrote of the power of prayer:

> All hell is vanquished when the believer bows his knee in importunate supplication. Beloved brethren, let us pray. We cannot all argue, but we can all pray; we cannot all be leaders, but we can all be pleaders; we cannot all be mighty in rhetoric, but we can all be prevalent in prayer. I would sooner see you eloquent with God than with men. Prayer links us with the Eternal, the Omnipotent, the Infinite, and hence it is our chief resort. . . . Be sure that you are with God, and then you may be sure that God is with you.[31]

Former seminary dean Thom Rainer cited statistical evidence regarding the power of prayer: "A study of churches that were previously plateaued or declining but now experiencing growth revealed a fascinating statistic. The report concluded that 71% of these churches reported an increased emphasis on prayer over the past several years as compared to only 40% of churches which continue on the plateau."[32] Such prayer does not happen without the leadership of the pastor. A Christian leader must continue to grow and lead in the discipline of prayer.

Full of Faith

Second, the leader demonstrates spiritual growth when he is "faith-filled." Spurgeon wrote, "I might say, the first, second, third, and last thing is faith. 'Without faith, it is impossible to please God'; and, if we are pleasing God, it is not by our talent, but by our faith."[33] The danger exists for one to become more confident in one's own abilities rather than continuing to trust and depend on God. Spurgeon believed that "dependence upon God is the flowing fountain of success."[34] Great spiritual leaders recognize their consistent need to rely on the Lord. Noted author Elmer Towns reinforces this axiom: "All great leaders have one common spiritual gift—faith."[35]

Spurgeon did not view faith as something exceptional for a leader but as a natural function in the Christian life: "Faith in God is sanctified common sense."[36] It is taking God at His word. "To believe God's Word is the most reasonable thing we can do; it is the plainest course that we can take, and the safest policy that we can adopt, even as to taking care of ourselves. . . . Let us stake all upon the faithfulness of God, and we shall never be ashamed or con-founded, world without end."[37]

Faith involves risk. Pastor Gene Getz writes, "Faith is reflected in Christians who are willing to step out and believe God's promises."[38] Spurgeon declared "We should have more faith. We need to believe more intensely in God, so as to trust Him more practically and more unquestioningly."[39] Spurgeon believed faith leads to accomplishments: "Let us attempt great things, for those who believe in the Name of the Lord succeed beyond all expectation. By faith, the worker lives."[40]

Led by the Spirit

Third, the leader demonstrates spiritual growth by a ministry that is Spirit-led. Spurgeon wrote: "I do not believe that God will set His seal to a ministry which does not aim at being strictly in accordance with the mind of the Spirit."[41] Those who are led by the Spirit will exhibit sensitivity to God's guidance through His Word. The conviction of sin and the convincing of righteousness and the judgment to come are all communicated through the agency of the Holy Spirit. The inspiration, illumination, and interpretation that issue from the revealed truth is confirmed by the Spirit. Spurgeon declared, "You must be with the Holy Ghost if you are to have the Holy Ghost with you."[42] A developing leader continues to grow as he is filled by the Holy Spirit and sensitive to the ongoing leadership of the Spirit.

Over time, the Christian leader, as he gets immersed in the work and finds that the routine becomes mundane and predictable, might become dulled to the leading of the Spirit. He also might resist the proddings of the Holy Spirit regarding his personal devotion and fresh attention to God's Word. The leader, however, who continues to grow in faithfulness and response to God's guid-ance will seek continual renewal of his commitment to Christ. To that end, Spurgeon wrote, "Nothing can maintain us in the freshness of our beginnings but the daily anointing of the Spirit."[43]

Servant Leadership

Fourth, the leader demonstrates spiritual growth by a lifestyle that is ser-vant driven. Thus, he manifests "a more thorough spirit of self-sacrifice."[44] Many Christian leaders have sacrificed more lucrative careers as they answered a call to vocational ministry. The demands of the ministry and the burdens of financial limitations have created practical lifestyle difficulties for pastors and their families. Fortunately, many churches have recognized the need to support their pastors and staff by a standard that now typically matches that of the average lay leader. But the call to self-sacrifice for a leader goes beyond financial and material sacrifice.

The attitude of self-sacrifice includes the discipline of dying daily to self to live to Christ. Spurgeon wrote, "We must be prepared to give up everything else: our name, our repute, our friendships, our connections, must all go without reserve, if Christ needs them."[45] The Christian leader is not concerned primarily with personal comforts and preferences but with doing that which brings honor and glory to Christ. Spiritual growth in this area means that one is becoming increasingly more conformed to the image of Christ. Spurgeon's words remind us, "Let us fear no loss, because we have nothing to lose, seeing that all we possess is Christ's already."[46] As a leader surrenders continuously all areas of his life to the Lord, he will experience a greater sense of satisfaction in his service to Christ.

The leader who surrenders his all to God and does not hold back any area of his life will bear true spiritual fruit. His holy pursuit and spiritual growth is like an offering given to God. As Spurgeon so notably stated, "We have given ourselves up to the work of God, and we cannot go back. We desire to be whole burnt offerings and complete sacrifices to God, and we dare not shun the altar."[47]

SPURGEON'S LEADERSHIP LESSONS

- **A Christian leader must first be led by God before he can lead others.** The principal foundation of Spurgeon's leadership was his life of faith, based on his personal relationship to Jesus Christ. "Brethren, you are not meant for anything but God; therefore, surrender yourselves to God, and find in Him your wealth, your honour, and your all."
- **"An ounce of personal testimony is worth more than a ton of heavy theology."** Spurgeon's spiritual conversion was so profound that it became the primary motivation of his life as a Christian leader. From that time, his commitment was to witness to the salvation he experienced, that others might be brought to saving faith in Jesus Christ.
- **A good leader is true to his theological convictions.** Spurgeon's willingness to part company with his family over the issue of baptism as a teenager was indicative of the manner in which he always approached matters of faith. If he were convinced that something was correct according to the Scriptures, Spurgeon was willing to stand alone against those who differed with him.
- **A leader's effectiveness stems directly from one's spiritual commitment.** Spurgeon was convinced that the nature of a leader's own faith commitment determines his effectiveness in ministry. "True and genuine piety is necessary as the first indispensable requisite; whatever 'call' a man may pretend to have, if he has not been called to holiness, he certainly has not been called to the ministry."
- **Leaders persevere**. Spurgeon believed that Christian leaders should persevere in their calling. He decried those who left the ministry for other pursuits: "For us to turn aside from our life-work, and to seek distinction elsewhere, is absolute folly; a blight will be upon us, we shall not succeed in anything but the pursuit of God's glory."
- **A leader will not take you farther than he's gone himself.** Spurgeon believed that continued spiritual development is essential for increased effectiveness in leadership. "Let this be the burning passion of your souls. *Grow to be leaders and champions.*"
- **Spiritual growth is the measure of a leader's continued impact on his followers.** Spurgeon demonstrated his commitment to spiritual growth as a leader in four different areas—by being prayer empowered, faith filled, Spirit led, and servant driven. "Be sure that you are with God, and then you may be sure that God is with you."

5

CHARACTER

An Example of Integrity

*Let us aspire to saintliness of spirit and character. I am
persuaded that the greatest power we can get over our fellow
men is the power which comes of consecration and holiness.*[1]

The personal characteristics of a leader bear witness to the lasting influence
of that leader. Throughout his extended ministry, C. H. Spurgeon exhibited
steadfastly the highest moral conduct in his personal and public life. James
Douglas wrote in his biography of Spurgeon, "He was great as a man . . . great
in private with God, and great in public with his fellow men."[2] The man had a
lifelong consistency, and his influence helped to lead thousands of people to
follow the Christ he loved and served.

The Issue of Character

The issue of character is debated hotly in leadership circles today. Tradi-
tionally, *character* has been defined as the "moral constitution of a person."
Popular descriptions today are "what you are when no one is looking" or "who
you are in the dark." In other words, character reveals the true substance of a
person—who that person really is, day in and day out, in good times and bad
times—over the course of a lifetime. Contrary to some opinions, character is
not one's title, role, or position.

John Hawkins of Leadership Edge expands on that idea: "In its essence,
leadership is not a position, it's a lifestyle."[3] Those who have made the greatest
mistakes are leaders who have assumed that their position was more important than their lifestyle. For some of them, the consequences have been tragic.

Some years ago, America dealt with the sexual improprieties that occurred by President Bill Clinton with an intern in the White House. A resulting impeachment trial did not lead to any conviction, but perhaps a greater verdict was rendered to the nation. The notion that character was essential to leadership was muted by the message sent that popularity and prosperity had become the defining measures of a good leader.

Counter to aberrant popular notions, business leader/consultant Warren Bennis contends that character is the "essence of leadership."[4] Leaders cannot lead unless they have the full trust of their followers. When that trust is betrayed, support is withdrawn. Trusted leaders seek to be consistent in their lives publicly and privately, are authentic in their concern for their followers, and are true to their word.

Spurgeon's Stellar Contrast

Given the stellar character that Spurgeon demonstrated through his life, questions about his character almost seem moot. Upon his arrival in London at the age of nineteen, Spurgeon became an instant sensation as the crowds thronged to hear him preach at New Park Street Baptist Church. His quick rise in popularity drew the critical attention of both the secular and the religious press, who vilified him for his unconventional methods and style of preaching. He was lampooned as a country bumpkin from Essex whom the media elite considered uncouth and "vulgar." He was caricatured in many early cartoons as a charlatan seeking fame and fortune in the city. These characterizations comprised what came to be known as "the media controversy."[5]

People scoffed at his preaching, questioned his motives, lambasted his ego, and ridiculed his ambitions. But in all of the public debate about Spurgeon's early ministry, never was a question raised concerning moral impropriety. In fact, as Spurgeon's ministry matured, the secular press generally came to respect him for the many moral contributions that he made through his pulpit, his church, and his notable philanthropic enterprises. Their later treatment of him was a stark contrast to their suspicions of him in the early days. No doubt, the changes occurred because Spurgeon earned their trust in demonstrating a public persona that was matched by a pattern of private behavior.

How different Spurgeon's world seems from our world today, where leering paparazzi and ravenous news reporters seem to lurk around every corner, all too eager to uncover the latest scandal that will expose another immoral leader. The secular press of our day gives little deference to anyone's office or position in its quest for a story. Rather, its insatiable appetite for the sordid and the scurrilous serves its suspect motives to satisfy the feeding frenzy of a public that demands such reporting. The end result is a "dumbing down" of the expectations of public leaders, with moral accountability becoming quickly a mere shadow of the past.

Development of Character

The crisis of character that we now see has occurred in both the secular realm and the religious realm. Unfortunately, more often than not, the reports of immorality among leaders are true. We have come to expect such revelations, which only feeds the cynicism of those who have come to believe that all leaders are morally compromised. We hear reports about pastors running off with their secretaries, television evangelists having indiscriminate trysts with call girls, corporate executives securing apartments to keep their lovers in a lifestyle of comfort in various cities—and even presidents having sexual liaisons with young interns in the Oval Office.

To make the right case for character regarding leadership, one must consider the consistency of one's actions, the motives behind one's decisions, the behavior in one's relationships, the integrity of one's employment of ethical principles, and certainly one's authenticity in lifestyle. But true character cannot be evaluated properly in the span of a few years or even several decades. To judge one's character, especially as it relates to leadership, a full accurate assessment could take a lifetime. A leader might exhibit stellar character in his leadership today, but tomorrow he might fall.

Christian Vulnerability

Christian leaders are just as vulnerable as secular leaders in seeking to maintain the high moral conduct expected of them. Pastor Jack Hayford contends that a "heart quest" is what determines the consistent daily pursuit of Christlike character. "The development of leadership character takes more than the practice of external disciplines, for it involves the heart, not just habits."[6] For Spurgeon, that quest began in his early childhood. Under the tutelage of a godly family, especially his grandparents, his character was influenced and developed in a way that would bring a lifetime of honor to Christ.

Stambourne, the home of Spurgeon's godly Puritan grandfather, had a sin-

gular attraction for the young man. There, under his grandfather's training and
tutelage, the foundation of Spurgeon's character was laid, and the seed was sown
that was in later years to bring forth such an abundant harvest. His parents were
blessed with seventeen olive branches to adorn their home; and with but scant
means for their support, it was doubtless a great relief to them for their firstborn
to make, in a large measure, his grandfather's parsonage his home.[7]

As a young boy, Spurgeon lived for extended periods of time with his grandparents. Their moral influence made an indelible and life-long impression
upon him. They taught him the importance of honesty and integrity, and modeled the example of Christian righteousness. Spurgeon took to heart what he
learned from his grandparents and built upon the foundation he received in
his childhood. It served as a basis for the character he developed and maintained throughout his ministry.

Character Personified

What made the difference for Spurgeon? Was he a perfect man? Did he not
experience the temptations of other men? Was it easier for him than it is for
leaders today because of the times in which he lived?

The Victorian era certainly was a time of high public morality in leadership.
Prudish behavior was the popular icon of conduct for the elite, the educated,
and the cultured. Queen Victoria set the standard that prompted her subjects
to emulate her. No doubt, the moral tone that she set raised the bar for all leaders of the day. And yet, even in a time when high morality was supposedly the
standard, Spurgeon was not naive enough to ignore his own vulnerability. He
was the first to admit his own sinfulness before a righteous God and a watching world. His sermons are full of the recognition of his own plight were he
not transformed by the abounding grace of his Savior. Spurgeon's secret to
overcoming sinful temptation was nothing less than his total submission to
the rule and reign of Christ in his life. Through his unwavering commitment,
strong convictions, and disciplined lifestyle, Spurgeon's character remained
avowedly consistent with the faith he professed.

Above Temptation?

Undoubtedly, Spurgeon experienced temptation. The esteem and trust that
he held throughout his ministry was not earned in a day but gained over

time. The reputation that Spurgeon enjoyed at the Metropolitan Tabernacle could have become tarnished easily had their pastor succumbed to many of the temptations that no doubt came his way. Because Spurgeon traveled extensively throughout his ministry, his behavior and associations were open to public speculation. But no question ever arose regarding his personal conduct in all of his many journeys. Spurgeon also could have compromised his reputation in other ways. As the entrepreneur of many enterprises including the orphanage, almshouses, and other benevolent ministries, Spurgeon could have padded his own pockets at the expense of those organizations. But the evidence is quite clear that, instead, he gave sacrificially to fill the coffers of those groups, never profiting from them personally. As the leading pastor in London, Spurgeon could have sought to wield his influence and power over his contemporaries such as to embellish his own reputation. But, to the contrary, he was more often prone to take unpopular stands as a matter of personal conviction that proved rather costly in his associations. Observing his track record, one would find it difficult to accuse him of seeking to curry public favor or personal prestige, especially at the risk of moral compromise.

Keeping Tight Reins

As far as his ministry at the Metropolitan Tabernacle, Spurgeon kept fairly tight reins on the leadership circles of his church and its extended ministries. He selected his associates carefully, including the appointment of his own brother, James Archer Spurgeon, as his pastoral assistant. James helped to administer the ongoing activities and daily ministries of the church. With such trusted leadership around Charles, it is not surprising that no hint arose of any type of immoral scandal or unethical dealings by those who were in leadership with him. One has to believe that Spurgeon's own example of strict personal discipline, combined with the high expectations and accountability of those who assisted him in ministry, staved off the types of problems that unfortunately have become more frequent in religious organizations today.

The Model of Character

People today want to know that their leaders are credible, that they can be trusted. Members of an evangelical church want to see their pastor exhibit the personal qualities that he expounds from the pulpit—for example, that their pastor is a truthful leader who keeps his word. They want to know that he is honest in all of his dealings, pays his bills on time, doesn't cheat on his taxes, and follows through with his commitments. They want not only to see him speak about evangelism but also to know that he is an evangelist personally. They don't want just to hear preaching on tithing; they want to know that their pastor is a biblical giver. They need to know that when he challenges them to be involved in daily ministry, he, too, is doing his part. They want to see their pastor demonstrate family priorities, not just proclaim what the Bible teaches about them. They desire to hear about God's love, but they want to see their leader practice love. They need to hear about godly priorities, but they want to see their pastor demonstrate the right balance in his own lifestyle.

Uncompromising in Standards

How did Spurgeon rise to the challenge in modeling character, especially regarding leadership? He made his case for character not only in words but also in the context of his daily life. His primary focus was the preaching of the gospel and the ministries that were an extension of that calling—to lead believers in matters of the faith. Spurgeon championed the cause for authentic leaders to exhibit an uncompromising standard of moral character. He believed that the most effective leadership is by example, not by edict. The model of godliness that a Christian leader exhibits challenges others to follow Christ through the testimony of a leader's life. First Peter 2:21 says, "To this you were called, because Christ suffered for you, leaving you an example, that you should follow in his steps" (NIV). Spurgeon wrote about the inevitability of followers looking to their leaders:

> I do not think that any of us would dare to say to our people, "follow me in all things." And yet their tendency is to follow the pastor. In this tendency lies influence for the holy, and a dreadful power for mischief for the careless. Many beginners take readily to an earthly model; they find it more natural to copy a godly man, whom they have seen, than to imitate the Lord Jesus whom they have not seen. I do not commend them in this; but so it is, and we must be tender toward this weakness so that it may not become the occasion of evil.[8]

A "Safe Example"

Spurgeon's awareness of the dependence of his followers upon his model made him extremely aware of his influence upon them. His desire was to be a "safe example" as a Christian leader: "It is a shocking state of things when good people say, 'Our minister undoes in the parlour what he has done in the pulpit; he preaches very well, but his life does not agree with his sermons.' . . . God help us so to live that we may be safe examples to our flocks."[9]

In Spurgeon's day, an occasional public incident occurred in which pastors failed to lead by example. It troubled him greatly when he observed the open contradictions of a leader's "walk and talk" in his professed faith. He had very little patience with leaders who did not seem to care about the inconsistencies of their public proclamations and personal lifestyle. When a minister fell, Spurgeon believed that the person could be restored spiritually, but at the same time that person evidenced a weakness that spelled trouble. He shared with his students his belief: "Open immorality, in most cases, however deep the repentance, is a fatal sign that ministerial graces were never in the man's character."[10] He believed that ministers must be on their guard lest they fall victim to sin: "Self-indulgence has slain its thousands. Let us have every passion and habit under due restraint; if we are not masters of ourselves, we are not fit to be leaders in the Church of Christ."[11] He continued regarding leaders, "We have need of very vigorous piety, because our danger is so much greater than that of others."[12]

J. C. Ryle echoes Spurgeon's sentiments: "Doctrine is useless if it is not accompanied by a holy life. It is worse than useless; it does positive harm. Something of 'the image of Christ' must be seen and observed by others in our private life, and habits, and character, and doings."[13]

Breech of Fellowship

One example of Spurgeon's high moral standards was the subsequent rift that occurred between him and Joseph Parker over an issue that Spurgeon believed to be a compromise of Christian conduct. Parker was pastor of the City Temple, a large London church comparable to the Metropolitan Tabernacle. Parker and Spurgeon were ministerial colleagues and friends who cooperated in various evangelistic and ministerial efforts in the city for several decades. But in the latter years of Spurgeon's ministry his amicable association with Parker came into question when he discovered that Parker frequented the secular theaters of London. Spurgeon believed the theater to be a bastion of immorality that represented the evils of the world. He could not fathom Parker's support for such worldly amusements. Parker responded to Spurgeon's criticism and castigation by writing him an open letter that was published in London newspapers. The rift was never mended before Spurgeon's death. One wonders how many of our Christian leaders today, given the level of compromise that has become the norm regarding popular forms of entertainment, would give a second thought to Spurgeon's challenge.

The Influence of Character

Oswald Sanders defined leadership as "influence," a definition that John Maxwell has popularized. The more influence a person has over others, the more they will follow his leadership. What's true in the secular world in this case is true in the Christian world as well. Christian leaders, above all, must demonstrate moral character if they expect to exert lasting influence upon their followers. People lose faith in their leaders when their morals are compromised. Spurgeon used the phrase "greatest power" to describe the influence that a leader could have over his followers: "Let us aspire to saintliness of spirit and character. I am persuaded that the greatest power we can get over our fellow-men is the power which comes of consecration and holiness."[14]

Moral Failure in Leadership

The greatest power or influence a leader can have over someone is through his "saintliness of spirit and character." Spurgeon believed that the closer one got to Christ and the more obedient one became to the truths revealed in God's Word, the greatest power for good existed in that person's life. The Rev. Jesse Jackson, noted religious and political leader, challenged that belief. Jackson was found to have fathered a child out of wedlock. When it became public knowledge two years later, Jackson was asked whether his moral influence had been compromised. Jackson responded that he did not think that his moral leadership had been affected. Indeed, shortly after the revelation of Jackson's immoral conduct, a seventy-one-year-old lady at the church where he attended worship declared, "We stand behind him. He is a great leader no matter what."[15]

Spurgeon, one suspects, would have been inclined otherwise. "When we hear of a man who has ruined his character by a surprising act of folly," he wrote, "we may surmise, as a rule, that this mischief was but one sulphurous jet from a soil charged with volcanic fire; or, to change the figure, one roaring lion from a den of wild beasts."[16]

Spurgeon lamented the occasions when public leaders experienced moral failure. He stated, "Alas, the open beard of reputation once shorn is hard to grow again."[17] Granted, some people have admitted public moral failings and have regained some measure of their leadership. But, for the most part, a public leader who is found to have committed immoral acts never achieves the same level of trust and confidence that he once enjoyed. The opportunity for influence, for the greatest power, is diminished when character is compromised.

Unity in Character

Integral to the character issue is the word *integrity*. An oft-quoted statement is "Image is what people think we are; integrity is what we really are."

Leadership expert Peter Drucker reported the results of a survey of thirteen hundred senior corporate executives. The survey revealed that integrity is the human quality most necessary to business success. Seventy-one percent of the respondents put it at the top of a list of sixteen traits responsible for enhancing an executive's effectiveness. If that is true of the secular world, it should be even more so in the religious world. C. B. Hogue wrote, "Most leaders, both spiritual and secular, list integrity as essential to effectiveness. It is one of the most important—if not *the* most important—characteristics in the development of spiritual leadership."[18]

Integrity is defined as "the state of being complete, unified." A leader with integrity is "incorruptible, honest, and dependable."[19] He does what he says he will do; he keeps his promises. When one has integrity, he has neither divided loyalties nor pretense. He has no duplicity or hypocrisy. As Bud Paxson writes, "Integrity speaks of persons who have integrated their inner and outer selves. They are on the inside what they appear to be on the outside."[20] Such a person has nothing to hide, nothing to fear.

Spurgeon referred to it as "integrity of spirit." He viewed integrity as utterly essential in the work of the ministry:

Dear brethren, we must acquire certain moral faculties and habits, as well as put aside their opposites. He will never do much for God who has not integrity of spirit. If we be guided by policy, if there be any mode of action for us but that which is straightforward, we shall make shipwreck before long. Resolve, dear brethren, that you can be poor, that you can be despised, that you can lose life itself, but that you cannot be a crooked thing. For you, let the only policy be honesty.[21]

Vanishing Commodities

Sadly, integrity and honesty are vanishing commodities today. Personal standards are deteriorating in a world obsessed by pursuing personal gratification and looking for shortcuts to success. Spurgeon believed that ethical behavior is fundamental. He proclaimed in his sermon titled "The Broken Fence," "Dare to be singular. Resolve to keep close to Christ. Make a stern determination to permit nothing in your life, however gainful or pleasurable, if it would dishonor the name of Jesus. Be dogmatically true, obstinately holy, immovably honest, desperately kind, fixedly upright."[22]

A leader with integrity does the right thing the right way for the right reason. He is a person of conviction. The Christian leader has consistent standards and high values that are patterned after Christ. Such a leader can be trusted. He has earned respect. He exercises self-discipline and self-control. John Maxwell calls this "the price tag of leadership." Engstrom and Dayton speak of the price of maintaining integrity:

> It often costs a great deal to maintain integrity, to keep our commitments. Sometimes it may cost the organization a great deal to do it just because we said we would. Many times it is easier to conclude that we had better let this one slip because the extra expense involved will really stress us. When that happens, we lost some of our integrity.[23]

The Legacy of Character

Spurgeon warned his students, "The highest moral character must be sedulously maintained."[24] The diligence to which Spurgeon applied himself to the highest moral standards gave credence to the whole spectrum of his influence as a Christian leader. The legacy he left was rich in many ways but especially regarding character. He believed that godly character was the best testimony one could leave behind. He concluded, "A good character is the best tombstone. Those who loved you, and were helped by you, will remember you when forget-me-nots are withered. Carve your name on hearts, and not on marble."

Toward that goal, each leader should pray as Spurgeon prayed:

> As you would, on your bended knees, cry day and night that no moral catastrophe may occur to you, beware of the sin which leads to it, beware of the backsliding which culminates in it; for if we have not the cause, the effect will not follow. The Lord will preserve us if, day by day, we cry unto Him to cleanse our way.[25]

SPURGEON'S LEADERSHIP LESSONS

- **Authentic leaders exhibit an uncompromising standard of moral character.** It is no coincidence that Spurgeon's legacy as a Christian leader is due in large measure to the fact that he exhibited steadfastly the highest moral conduct throughout his life.
- **The early development of character is crucial to the moral constitution of a leader.** Under the training and tutelage of godly Puritan grandparents, the foundation of Spurgeon's character was laid, and the seed was sown that was in later years to bring forth such an abundant harvest.
- **A leader demonstrates consistency in the moral conduct of his personal and public life.** Throughout his extended ministry, Spurgeon's life evidenced such consistency. James Douglas wrote in his biography of Spurgeon, "He was great as a man . . . great in private with God, and great in public with his fellow men."
- **The most effective moral leadership is by example, not by edict.** Spurgeon championed the cause for authentic leaders to exhibit an uncompromising standard of moral character. He wrote, "God help us so to live that we may be safe examples to our flocks."
- **The model of godliness exhibited by a Christian leader challenges others to follow Christ through the testimony of the leader's life.** People are drawn to Christ when they see a leader live what he professes. Spurgeon was instrumental in leading thousands of people to faith through his ministry.
- **The degree to which a leader is trusted will determine the degree of his influence upon his followers.** Spurgeon wrote, "Let us aspire to saintliness of spirit and character. I am persuaded that the greatest power we can get over our fellow-men is the power which comes of consecration and holiness."
- **Leaders will experience temptation like anyone else, but the difference lies in how they respond to such temptation.** Spurgeon's secret to overcoming sinful temptations was his personal relationship to Christ. Through his unwavering commitment, strong convictions, and disciplined lifestyle, Spurgeon's character was avowedly consistent with the faith he professed.
- **The responsibility of leadership demands constant vigilance regarding one's conduct.** Spurgeon realized the perilous effect that immoral behavior could have on kingdom efforts: "We have need of very

vigorous piety, because our danger is so much greater than that of others."

- **Leaders who succumb to moral failure will find it difficult to lead effectively again.** Spurgeon lamented, "Alas, the open beard of reputation once shorn is hard to grow again. Open immorality, in most cases, however deep the repentance, is a fatal sign that ministerial graces were never in the man's character."

- **Integrity is a core determination of true leadership.** A leader with integrity does the right things the right way for the right reason. Spurgeon charged, "Dear brethren, we must acquire certain moral faculties and habits, as well as put aside their opposites. He will never do much for God who has not integrity of spirit."

- **Self-discipline/self-control makes up "the price tag of leadership."** Spurgeon took costly stands, which reflected his moral principles based on his conviction that "The highest moral character must be sedulously maintained."

- **The personal characteristics of a leader bear witness to the lasting influence of that leader.** Spurgeon testified, "A good character is the best tombstone. Those who loved you, and were helped by you, will remember you when forget-me-nots are withered. Carve your name on hearts, and not on marble."

PART TWO

Leading Through
the Seasons

6

CASTING VISION

Spurgeon's Goals and Planning

*No mortal hath fully seen God's glory as yet, and the Divine
Spirit waits to lead you by study and prayer to a yet clearer
vision of the deep things of God.*[1]

Effective leaders are able to create and sustain a compelling vision for their
followers.[2] When Ed Young Sr. became pastor of Second Baptist Church in
Houston, he realized the need to have a compelling vision for the growth and
ministry of his church. God gave him a vision of thousands of people coming onto the properties of their church every day. His vision took on practical
direction when he established a county-wide church softball league, building
multiple ball fields to host the league on their church grounds. Hundreds of
people came to play softball at Second Baptist, and many of them came to faith
in Jesus Christ as Lord and Savior. Through side-door evangelism, the church
established their vision by sharing the gospel on the ball fields of Houston.[3]

His son, Ed Young Jr., himself a noted church pastor in Houston, addressed
the need for leaders to maintain a "vertical vision": "Growing up as a pastor's
son, serving on a church staff, and then planting a church, I've seen the ministry from many angles. And I've noticed that godly leaders catch their vision
vertically, from God. When they apply this passionately and creatively, people
are reached for the glory of God."[4] Like father, like son.

Similarly, C. H. Spurgeon's "vertical vision" was to lead a declining church in
the heart of London to renewed growth and service in its community, reaching
thousands of people with the gospel of Christ. Like the Youngs in Houston,
Spurgeon in London found practical ways to realize his vision, launching a
multifaceted evangelistic enterprise that enabled his church to grow from two

hundred to more than five thousand members during his ministry there. As the vision unfolded, the ministries multiplied, and the church's influence extended beyond London to the rest of England and to much of the Western world.

The Necessity of Vision

Leaders and organizations must have a vision to survive and thrive in the twenty-first century. Although we agree that the Great Commission (Matt. 28:19–20) is the overall vision that Jesus gave to us all—to take the gospel to the ends of the earth—it is still imperative for each local church to discover a unique way that that vision is to be implemented through the local body of Christ.

The spiritual insight from Proverbs continues to provide a divine demarcation: "Where there is no vision, the people perish" (29:18 KJV). Numerous churches and organizations are hanging by their thumbnails today in an effort to stay alive. Some of them are dying because of a failed vision or the lack of a vision. Many of them are well intentioned in their efforts, but somewhere along the way they lost their vitality and dynamism because they lost their vision. Perhaps they became content with things as they were and sought to "maintain the status quo" of the organization when the status quo was nothing worth maintaining. To move a group forward in growth and achievement requires leadership based on vision. Helen Keller, who overcame deafness and blindness to lead an incredible life, especially knew the importance of vision. She lamented that, "The most pathetic person in the world is someone who has sight but has no vision."[5]

What is vision? Jonathan Swift said, "Vision is the art of seeing things invisible."[6] In the context of leadership, the leader must be able to see what the followers cannot see. Leroy Eims describes it thus: "A leader is one who sees more than others see, who sees farther than others see, and who sees before others do."[7] In other words, the leader has an extraordinary perception regarding the organization's prospects. George Barna calls it "a clear mental portrait of the future."[8] Spurgeon believed that clear vision is essential. He shared with his students, "It is but a defect of our vision that we cannot see things correctly."[9]

Casting Vision

What is contained in the leader's ability to cast vision? First, the leader must have a firm grasp of the vision that God has given him. Then he must seek to implement it in the organization. John Maxwell emphasizes the leader's role in communicating his vision: (1) see it clearly, (2) say it continuously, and (3) show it creatively. The leader must have a crystal clear view of the future that has been revealed to him. Then he must endeavor to communicate it as frequently as the opportunity affords itself. Rick Warren states that he must repeat the church's stated vision to the congregation every twenty-six days to keep it before his members. The leader shows the vision creatively through proclamation, presentation, publicity, testimony, and visual media—whatever it takes to get the message through to the people.

A President Remembered

The movie *Nixon* includes a scene in which President Nixon goes down to the kitchen of the White House late at night and in the process wakens his Cuban chef. After a little small talk, they get into a serious conversation of a personal nature. Nixon asks the Cuban if America made it hard for his people. The chef replies that not Nixon, but President Kennedy, has made it hard for them (referring to hardships that came after the failed "Bay of Pigs" invasion in 1961 and the subsequent embargo). Then Nixon asks him if he remembers what he was doing when Kennedy was killed.

The Cuban replied, "Yes."

Nixon asked him, "Did you cry?"

He said, "Yes."

Nixon asked, "Why?"

The chef answered, "Because Kennedy made us look up to the stars."

As portrayed in the film, the Cuban, like many young people of that generation, was inspired by the vision of a "New Frontier" that the young president proposed. His challenge to America to put a man on the moon within a decade set in motion the accomplishment of a worthwhile goal that contributed to his legacy:

> I believe this nation should commit itself to achieving the goal, before this decade is out, of landing a man on the moon and returning him safely to the earth. No single space project in this period will be more impressive to mankind, or more important for the long-range exploration of space; and none will be so difficult or expensive to accomplish.[10]

That goal was realized when Neil Armstrong became the first man to set his foot on the moon in July 1969. It would not have occurred without a vision.

What Vision Accomplishes

Once the leader grasps the vision, he bears the responsibility for causing the organization to grasp the same vision. He becomes the pacesetter for accomplishing the vision. He finds creative means to lead the group to develop the same passion that he displays for the vision. The members of the group become inspired with the innate desire to follow their leader, to go where they have never been.

What will this kind of vision accomplish? First, such vision inspires. It brings people together for a common purpose. That purpose must be larger than any one person—it must be something that a group can accomplish *only* with God's help. Second, vision instructs. It guides our decisions. Third, vision interprets. It helps to clarify options/priorities. As Bennis and Nanus state: "The leader's vision for the organization must be clear, attractive, and attainable. We tend to trust leaders who create these visions, since vision represents the context for shared beliefs in a common organizational purpose."[11]

Implementing Vision

Leadership is the capacity to translate vision into reality. The vision means little if it does not result in implementation.

C. H. Spurgeon had a clear vision of his purpose and calling in the ministry. His passion to preach the gospel became the flame that ignited his all-encompassing ministry. From the first time that he spoke at a little village church in Teversham in rural Cambridgeshire to his last sermon in the pulpit at the Metropolitan Tabernacle in London, he pursued the specific plan that God had given him—to preach the gospel to as many people as possible. He implemented his vision every chance he got. At all times, in every way, in as many places as he could go, Spurgeon looked for opportunities to proclaim the saving message of Christ that was so dear to his heart. His personal motto, which became the motto of The Pastors' College, was *et teneo et teneor*—"I hold and am held." He described its application for him: "We labor to hold forth the cross of Christ with a bold hand among the sons of men, because that cross holds us fast by its attractive power. Our desire is, that every man may hold the truth, and be held by it; especially the truth of Christ crucified."[12]

Through the power of the message of the Cross, Spurgeon went to any length to bring the good news to all hearers. It was not unusual for him, especially in his earlier years in London, to preach seven to ten times a week. Whenever he could, and as his health allowed, he was always ready to preach, whether in a small chapel, in the open air, or to his own congregation. With that personal enthusiasm for getting out the message, he brought creative leadership to implementing his vision through not only his pastoral ministry but also other extensions beyond the local church. Although Spurgeon knew that the gospel would achieve its desired end, he also knew that he had to entrust to God the results of his efforts:

> If we do not see souls saved today or tomorrow, we will still work on. ... We are laboring for eternity, and we count not our work by each day's advance, as men measure theirs; it is God's work, and must be measured by His standard. Be ye well assured that, when time, and things created, and all that oppose themselves to the Lord's truth, shall be gone, every earnest sermon preached, and every importunate prayer offered, and every form of Christian service honestly rendered, shall remain embedded in the mighty structure which God from all eternity has resolved to raise to His own honor.[13]

People Respond to Vision

Some leaders do not see the crucial importance of vision. They believe that the key to organizational growth is simply to meet the needs of the people/ the customers, and the rest will take care of itself. Rick Warren, pastor of the thriving Saddleback Church in Southern California, offers a very different insight: "People respond to passionate vision, not need."[14] Through many different phases, and over an extended period of time, Warren implemented his vision of a purpose-driven church. The result was the creation of one of the largest churches in the world. But, as well, the influence of Warren's vision through the principles of the purpose-driven model have been recreated around the globe. It is a vision that focuses on the defining moment when God's Spirit moves through the church and empowers the people to respond to that vision as they engage in kingdom work. Needs still exist, but the vision becomes the driving force for focusing people on the powerful change of the gospel in their lives.

Sometimes the vision needs to be recast. Circumstances can change, and ministry directions might need to be altered. Also, even the best vision can become stale after a while and need to be reapplied. Living in a postmodern world, we deal with ever-changing twists and turns in an increasingly secular culture. With a fresh vision, a church or organization can rise to the latest challenges. Regardless of the hurdles, vision is the ability to see the opportunities within the current circumstances. Problems might arise, but folks become aware that they serve a great God who can do all things. People want to be part of something that is larger than themselves. When a leader has a vision and gives a group some noble purpose for which to strive, it becomes a rallying point for them to accomplish great things together.

Honoring the Past

Visionary leadership includes an effort to honor the best accomplishments of the past while adapting strategies and adjusting goals to provide growth for the future. It builds on tradition, and, at the same time, paves the way to accept change, explore new ideas, and foster creativity.

Spurgeon lauded the worthy leadership of his distinguished predecessors and built on their accomplishments. But he did not let the past become a stranglehold on his own unique vision. He sought to put church members to work according to their individual gifts while including them in the organizational vision. Visionary leadership, at its base, is the means for achieving the church's mission in its community and beyond.

Positive About the Future

A visionary leader is positive about the future because God has given a vision of that future. He is able to envision the possibilities. When Spurgeon went to New Park Street Baptist Church in London, as Professor Lewis Drummond notes, he "intuitively knew God had great things in store for the church and he must give them strong leadership."[15] Spurgeon's ministry was an extension of his forward-looking faith:

> In our Christian pilgrimage it is well, for the most part, to be look-
> ing forward. Forward lies the crown, and onward is the goal.
> Whether it be for hope, for joy, for consolation, or for the inspiring

of our love, the future must, after all, be the grand object of the eye of faith.[16]

Others Sharing the Vision

A spiritual leader must get godly people around him who share in the vision. Good leaders not only have vision but also are able to recruit, train, and deploy others to implement the vision. Too often, leaders try to accomplish their vision singlehandedly. Spurgeon was not so foolish. He surrounded himself with leaders who were able to help implement the vision for his ministry. As he founded The Pastors' College and The Stockwell Orphanage, pursued his writing ministry, embarked on his multifaceted philanthropic enterprises, and led in the continuing growth of the Metropolitan Tabernacle, his leadership was extended through the energies, skills, and abilities of well-equipped lay leaders. They multiplied Spurgeon's effectiveness as they carried out the ministries that he had envisioned.

No doubt, Spurgeon's practical implementation of his vision was adapted as his ministry experienced exponential growth, and adjustments had to be made along the way. The Metropolitan Tabernacle's multitude of ministries bore little resemblance to the congregation at New Park Street when Spurgeon first arrived in London.

Setting Goals

A visionary leader sets goals that enable his followers to accomplish great things as part of the organization. He sets goals to realize his vision. Goals give specific direction to the vision. Goals arise from a vision of what God is calling the individual to do. Spurgeon's goals were closely related to his clear calling to preach the gospel to as many people as God would give him strength to reach. That is why he maintained such a breakneck pace in preaching seven to ten times per week in the earlier years of his ministry, taking as many engagements as were offered him. He was determined to get the message of Christ out to the masses.

Defining Goals

What is a goal? A goal is a dream with a deadline. What about those who have no goals? They might have goals, although they are unaware of them.

Still, other leaders conduct their business, manage their organization, and preach at their church but have no real goals toward which they have set their sights. They are no more than caretakers, like the captain of a ship who feeds his crew but lets the ship float aimlessly on the sea. Perhaps some leaders are like Christopher Columbus: he didn't know where he was going, he didn't know where he was when he got there, he didn't know where he had been when he returned, and he used someone else's money to do it!

As the old axiom goes, "Aim at nothing, and you're sure to hit it." Leaders can be aimless, shiftless, wiling away precious time, if they don't have any real objectives. Goals are essential. As Geoffrey F. Abert declared, "The most important thing about having goals is having one."

When Spurgeon planned for the building of the Metropolitan Tabernacle, his goal was not a short-term goal of building a building. His goal was to build a church that would enable him to plant many more churches like it:

> We must build this Tabernacle strongly, I am sure, for our friends are always with us. . . . But our desire is, after we have fitted up our vestry, schools, and other rooms, that we shall be able to build other chapels. . . . I will not rest until the dark county of Surrey is covered with places of worship. I look on this Tabernacle as only the beginning; within the last six months, we have started two churches,—one in Wandsworth and the other in Greenwich, and the Lord has prospered them, the pool of baptism has often been stirred with converts. And what we have done in two places, I am about to do in a third, and we will do it, not for the third or the fourth, but for the hundredth time, God being our Helper. I am sure I may make my strongest appeal to my brethren, because we do not mean to build this Tabernacle as our nest, and then to be idle. We must go from strength to strength, and be a missionary church, and never rest until, not only this neighborhood, but our country, of which it is said that some parts are as dark as India, shall have been enlightened with the gospel.[17]

Spurgeon not only had a goal to build his church but also a goal to have it paid for by completion. "Now with regard to *our prospects*. We are to build this place, and the prospect I anticipate is, that it will be paid for before it is opened."[18] Through much prayer and effort, that goal was realized, and the Tabernacle was open with no debt remaining after its construction.

The Christian's Goal

What is the goal for Christian leaders? Ultimately, it is like what the apostle Paul wrote to the Corinthian church regarding his apostleship: "We make it our goal to please him" (2 Cor. 5:9 NIV). That goal becomes the all-encompassing aim of every Christian leader. It becomes the goal by which smaller goals come together to reach that main goal.

Leroy Eims shares the following three important reasons for setting goals:

1. Direction. The goal becomes the destination for pursuing direction in reaching it. If my goal is to go to Birmingham, I must know that it is Birmingham, Alabama, not Birmingham, England; otherwise, the directions to get there become very different.
2. Progress. Otherwise, there can be much activity, but no progress forward. A goal ensures that it's not just a lot of feverish activity but purposeful movement toward a goal.
3. Accomplishment. How can you know whether you've accomplished anything, if you have no real goal? The goal gives you a measure of what you have done in achieving success.[19]

The leader should not set goals arbitrarily. Goals must be relevant, reachable, and measurable.

Goals should be *relevant* (their accomplishment counts). They relate to the need of the church and community.

Goals should be *reachable* (they can be accomplished). Unrealistic pipe dreams and setting of ridiculous goals are counterproductive and produce much frustration. Setting ridiculous goals might hinder folks from setting goals again.

Goals should be *measurable* (time to accomplish them). Vague goals with no specific time frames have little effect. A system of accountability is necessary.

Goals Measure Faith

Goals are a direct measure of a leader's faith. Peter Wagner, a leader in church growth, calls goals "faith projections." He writes, "The overwhelming consensus of individuals whom God has blessed with large, growing churches is that it could never be done without the faith required to set goals."[20]

Spurgeon possessed a faith that enabled him to anticipate great progress and advancement in the ministries of his church. He stated boldly,

> We believe in a present God wherever we may be, and a working and operating God accomplishing His own purposes steadfastly and surely in all matters, places, and times; working out His designs as much in what seemeth evil as in that which is manifestly good; in all things driving on in His eternal chariot towards the goal which infinite wisdom has chosen, never slackening His pace nor drawing the rein, but for ever, according to the eternal strength that is in Him, speeding forward without pause.[21]

Goals that are challenging and realistic represent the larger goal toward which God is moving us in our service to Him. In the process, our practical goals can produce motivation and excitement. Satisfaction comes when we achieve things that bring glory to God. Worldly achievements bring short-lived contentment, but things that last for eternity give enduring satisfaction. We have fulfilled something that is bigger than ourselves.

People are hungering to be a part of a movement that makes a difference in their world. If those members can see real evidence that a church and its leadership are committed to new and challenging directions, enthusiasm will be natural and spontaneous. Goal-setting moves us toward the future. It's a way to refocus and to dream again.

Visionary Planning

Visionary leaders understand the importance of planning. Leaders who fail to plan are planning to fail. The adage has proved true more often than not: "Proper prior planning prevents pitifully poor performance." The right kind of planning helps to put feet to the vision that has been shared.

Some readers who were around in the 1960s might recall the Beatles' song, "Nowhere Man": "He's a real nowhere man, sitting in his nowhere land, making all his nowhere plans for nobody. Doesn't have a thing to do, knows not where he's going to, isn't he a bit like you and me?" The fatalistic song bemoaned purposeless existence. Although Spurgeon and the Beatles were all English, there the similarities end. The rock group's vision was about personal gain and worldly fame; Spurgeon's plan was to advance God's kingdom. Spurgeon put it thus:

We believe in a God of purposes and plans, who has not left a blind fate to tyrannize over the world, much less an aimless chance to rock it to and fro. We are not fatalists, neither are we doubters of providence and predestination. We are believers in a God "who worketh all things after the counsel of His own will."[22]

The Divine Plan

Spurgeon operated under the premise that God has a plan for every church, a design for every Christian organization, and a purpose for every group that seeks to honor Him. He was resolute about the positive purpose of God according to the Scriptures. "'For I know the plans I have for you,' declares the LORD, 'plans to prosper you and not to harm you, plans to give you hope and a future'" (Jer. 29:11 NIV). The biblical promise is a blessing to be discovered by any group that desires to seek first the kingdom of God and His righteousness. The plans will fall in line accordingly.

Peter Wagner cites the following six advantages to planning:

1. It increases efficiency. God's resources of time, energy, and money are best used for good stewardship.
2. It permits midcourse corrections.
3. It unites the team with a singular plan and vision. Each member of the team understands his or her role in the vision.
4. It helps measure effectiveness. Progress is measured according to the plans.
5. It makes accountability natural.
6. It can become a model to help others.[23]

Spurgeon believed that planning was important but that one must always recognize God's sovereign leading in any plans that one makes in this life. "In his heart a man plans his course, but the LORD determines his steps" (Prov. 16:9 NIV). Once we know God's plan for us, we are then free to pursue His plan for action as we seek to accomplish His purpose. Practically applied, we follow the adage "Plan your work; work your plan."

Spurgeon became irritated by those who would make elaborate plans but never get beyond the planning stage. He was a man of action! "It is idle to spend time in making and altering plans, and doing nothing else; the best plan for doing God's work is to do it."[24]

Managing and Leading

A difference exists between managing and leading. Managers provide the tools, methods, and personnel for a task. Leaders give vision, strategy, and inspiration. Spurgeon was definitely more a leader than a manager. For instance, although he founded a college to train pastors, he did not become the principal of that college. A suitable leader was secured for the institution, and it prospered. Once ideas were implemented, other people stepped in to assist in leading the various ministries that Spurgeon had envisioned.

Putting a plan into action is costly. Questions to be asked include the following: Are you willing to pay the price? Are you willing to do whatever is necessary? Are you willing to sacrifice?

The key to a plan for action is seeking to grow God's church His way, not ours. It will take much discernment, much prayer, great discipline, and patience. But, in due time, we will reap the harvest if we do not lose heart. Spurgeon's sentiments are indicated in the following lines, which he wrote:

> When the world my heart is rending
> With its heaviest storm of care,
> My glad thoughts to heaven ascending,
> Find a refuge from despair.
>
> Faith's bright vision shall sustain me
> Till life's pilgrimage is past;
> Fears may vex and troubles pain me,
> I shall reach my home at last.[25]

SPURGEON'S LEADERSHIP LESSONS

- **Leaders and organizations must have a vision to survive and thrive in an ever-changing world.** Spurgeon recognized the need for a new vision upon his arrival in London to serve as pastor of a declining inner-city church.
- **Effective leaders are able to create and sustain a compelling vision for their followers.** Spurgeon brought to his church creative leadership that extended throughout his thirty-seven years of ministry.
- **Visionary leadership includes an effort to honor the best accomplishments of the past while adapting strategies and adjusting goals to provide growth for the future.** Spurgeon honored the great pastors who had served before him and built upon their accomplishments.
- **Leadership is the capacity to translate vision into reality.** C. H. Spurgeon had a clear vision of his purpose and calling in ministry. His passion to preach the gospel became the springboard that launched his all-encompassing ministry.
- **A leader must gather around him godly people who share the vision.** Spurgeon surrounded himself with capable assistants and lay leaders who were able to help him implement the vision for his ministry.
- **A visionary leader is positive about the future because God has given a vision of that future.** "In our Christian pilgrimage it is well, for the most part, to be looking forward. Forward lies the crown, and onward is the goal. Whether it be for hope, for joy, for consolation, or for the inspiring of our love, the future must, after all, be the grand object of the eye of faith."
- **A visionary leader sets goals that enable his followers to accomplish great things for the organization.** Spurgeon's goals emanated from his clear calling to preach the gospel, a gospel that he believed extended ministry to the whole person.
- **Goals are a direct measure of a leader's faith.** Spurgeon's faith enabled him to anticipate great progress and advancement in the ministries of his church as he pursued his goals.
- **A visionary leader understands the importance of planning.** Spurgeon said, "We believe in a God of purposes and plans, who has not left a blind fate to tyrannize over the world, much less an aimless chance to rock it to and fro. . . . We are believers in a God 'who worketh all things after the counsel of His own will.'"

7

COURAGE

Standing for Righteousness, Scripture, and Sound Teaching

Learn always to discriminate between things that differ; . . .
Many run after novelties, charmed with every new thing;
learn to judge between truth and its counterfeits, and you
will not be led astray.[1]

The great challenge for many Christian leaders today is standing strong for the cause of righteousness. In an age of conciliation and compliance, many persons in leadership positions find it difficult to stay above the fray of wavering convictions. The secular pressures of political correctness, the insatiable desire for success, the fretful concern over job security, and the lack of principled confidence in one's beliefs—all contribute to a pattern of weak leadership. Researcher George Barna writes, "Surprisingly few people have the internal strength to stand up for what is right. We call this courage. God's leaders are always people of great courage."[2]

Strong in Convictions

Evangelist Billy Graham testified that "Courage is contagious. When a brave man takes a stand, the spines of others are stiffened."[3] People are inspired when their leaders show the willingness to risk everything for their beliefs. John Maxwell tells the story about a nineteenth-century circuit-riding preacher named Peter Cartwright. On one occasion when Cartwright was speaking, someone told him that President Andrew Jackson would be in attendance and advised Cartwright to keep his remarks inoffensive. Ignoring such counsel, Cartwright preached a bold message and then concluded, "I have been told that Andrew Jackson is in this congregation, and I have been asked to guard my remarks. What I must say is that Andrew Jackson will go to hell if he doesn't repent of his sin." Everyone expected that the shocking statement had offended the president. But as soon as the sermon was over, Jackson strode up to Cartwright and said, "Sir, if I had a regiment of men like you, I would whip the world."[4]

Confronting Baptismal Regeneration

C. H. Spurgeon was a leader who demonstrated the courage of his convictions. He not only ignited his congregation at the Metropolitan Tabernacle but also inspired a nation by the courageous stands he took for the cause of righteousness. He was not one to compromise or waffle when it came to important moral issues. Regardless of the personal consequences, Spurgeon refused to yield any ground whatsoever. If he encountered error, he would confront it. He challenged ministers, "We must not allow sin to go unrebuked. Yield in all things personal, but be firm where truth and holiness are concerned."[5]

On one notable occasion, Spurgeon demonstrated the courage of his convictions as he confronted the error he encountered in the Church of England. His challenge to the nation's denomination resulted in what came to be known as "the Baptismal Regeneration Controversy." Although he was a friendly colleague of many of its leaders, Spurgeon did not shirk from taking on his evangelical brethren in the Established Church. He believed that they subscribed to a prayer book that advocated the salvation of infants through the rite of baptism. His threefold sermon series on the topic set off a whirlwind of controversy as many churchmen reacted to his charges. But he would not be deterred. Spurgeon rallied his congregation and issued an appeal for "a band of men and women who are prepared to be singular, so long as to be singular is to be right ... men and women of bold, unflinching lion-like hearts, who love Christ first, and his truth next, and Christ and his truth beyond all the world."[6]

Willing to Stand Alone

Spurgeon was resolute when it came to matters of spirituality and one's Christian conduct. Because he was confident in his doctrinal beliefs and firmly grounded in the Scriptures, he was willing to stand alone if necessary when it came to the cause of righteousness. In doing so, Spurgeon exerted firm leadership and set a bold standard for his contemporaries and other leaders to follow. He counseled ministers to be bold and courageous:

> May you also possess *the grand moral characteristic of courage!* By this, I do not mean impertinence, impudence, or self-conceit; but real courage to do and say calmly the right thing, and to go straight on at all hazards, though there should be none to give you a good word. I am astonished at the number of Christians, who are afraid to speak the truth to their brethren. I thank God that I can say this— there is no member of my church, no officer of the church, and no man in the world, to whom I am afraid to say before his face what I would say behind his back. Under God, I owe my position in my own church to the absence of all policy, and the habit of always saying what I mean.[7]

A problem today is that many leaders are focused more on trying to please everyone around them than on standing for God's truth and thus pleasing Him. Such leaders are afraid of creating any waves lest they unnecessarily forfeit their hard-earned popularity, position of status, or influential power.

Spurgeon was concerned, first and foremost, with pleasing his Lord. He wrote of the essential aim of giving one's total allegiance to God: "There must be no holding back to please one person, no rushing forward to satisfy another, no moving an inch even to gratify the whole community. . . . To please our Lord, though it may seem very difficult, is an easier task than pleasing men."[8]

Spurgeon received his fair share of ridicule and criticism for his intransigent positions on various issues. Regardless of whether one agreed with his positions, one could admire his willingness to count the cost of doing that which he believed was right in God's sight. He counted it a singular honor to serve as a minister of the gospel, contending that the spiritual office of pastor was the highest calling on the face of the earth. For him, engaging people through preaching, teaching, counseling, and conversation—regarding eternal matters of the soul, made any other vocation/occupation pale in contrast. He wrote, "Our work is the most important under Heaven, or else it is sheer imposture. If you are not earnest in carrying out your Lord's instructions, He will give His vineyard to another; for He will not put up with those who turn His service into trifling."[9]

Indeed, the work of the ministry is so important to the kingdom that a leader must seek wisdom and discernment that comes from God. He will no doubt face many challenging issues along the way and must decide the ones for which he is willing to fight. Spurgeon wrote,

> Learn always to discriminate between things that differ . . . learn to judge between truth and counterfeits, and you will not be led astray. . . . Ask the Holy Spirit to give you the faculty of discerning between good and evil, so shall you conduct your flocks far from poisonous meadows, and lead them into safe pasturage.[10]

Sound in Theology

Principled confidence comes to the leader who is well-grounded in his theological beliefs. Spurgeon's system of belief was based on evangelical Calvinism, the system of his revered grandfather and the Puritans before him. Some of his contemporaries, proponents of the more liberal "new theology," believed that Spurgeon represented an archaic system that was out of touch with the needs of a more sophisticated populace. But Spurgeon was not interested in anything "new" if *new* meant any belief that would contradict the time-honored truths of Reformed thought. He believed in progress, but not at the expense of truth: "Is there to be no progress? Yes, within the lines of revealed truth; but there must be no departure from fixed principles."[11]

"Dynamic" Calvinism

Critics at the other end of the spectrum perceived that Spurgeon had changed his Calvinistic beliefs to accommodate his evangelistic zeal. His detractors did not understand Spurgeon's driving passion, his intention to reach as many souls for Christ as possible. In reality, he modified his system only to the extent that he was able to make a broader appeal in the presentation of the gospel. This modification made him unacceptable to the hyper-Calvinists (those who believed in a fatalistic predestination), and, at the same time, he was unsatisfactory to the Arminians (those who believed in complete freedom of will). Spurgeon's practical application of theology was somewhere between the two, what Professor Lewis Drummond labels "dynamic Calvinism."[12] This balance was evident in a sermon that Spurgeon titled "Plenteous Redemption":

Christ has redeemed the souls of all His people who shall ultimately be saved. To state it after the Calvinistic fashion, Christ has redeemed His elect; but since you do not know His elect until they are revealed, we will alter that, and say, Christ has redeemed all penitent souls; Christ has redeemed all believing souls; and Christ has redeemed the souls of all those who die in infancy, seeing it is to be received, that all those who die in infancy are written in the Lamb's book of life, and are graciously privileged by God to go at once to heaven, instead of toiling through this weary world.[13]

Although he did subscribe to a well-defined system of belief, Spurgeon did not condone complacency in the area of theological knowledge. He demonstrated his own belief in Christian learning and education by his voracious appetite for reading theological works. He advocated instruction for everyone who sought to become Christian leaders. His founding of The Pastors' College supported his belief in the need for theological training. He wanted men to be equipped and competent in their theology, to be confident in their system of belief, and to receive training for their practical ministry. He urged them,

Be well instructed in theology, and do not regard . . . those who rail at it because they are ignorant of it. Many preachers are not theologians, and hence the mistakes which they make. It cannot do any hurt to the most lively evangelist to be also a sound theologian, and it may often be the means of saving him from gross blunders.[14]

Theological Aberrations

Many contemporary leaders make the mistake of running after the latest theological nuance and, thus, compromise their basic convictions in the process. In recent years, mainstream evangelicalism has faced the challenges of liberal influences such as the Jesus Forum, which purported to authenticate but in actuality debunked the validity of Christ's statements as recorded in the four Gospels. At the other end of the spectrum, evangelical Christianity has withstood the onslaught of charismatic excesses, such as the Toronto Blessing. Holy laughter, barking like dogs, and spiritual upchucking were some of the manifestations that characterized a movement the underpinnings of which exposed a spurious theology. One writer who witnessed the theological devastation wrought by the importation of the Toronto Blessing into England lamented its affects:

> We therefore appeal to all preachers to undertake systematic ex-
> pository preaching of the Word of God. We believe that expound-
> ing the Scriptures will undoubtedly lay a good foundation for spirit
> revival in the nation, but it will also guard the church against error
> in days where there is a great onslaught on the truth.[15]

In Spurgeon's day, with the importation of biblical criticism from the Euro-
pean continent, evangelicals faced threats in the form of universalism (the idea that everyone would eventually be saved), the questioning of the doctrine of substitutionary atonement (the doctrine that Christ died vicariously for our sins), and the "downgrading" of the Scriptures (negating biblical authority through the use of undiscerning critical tools). These were weighty issues for the pastor of the Metropolitan Tabernacle, and he met them head-on. But he would not engage in scuffles over peripheral issues such as proposed theo-
ries about the details of Christ's second coming. For Spurgeon, the important issue was whether one believed in a literal return of Christ to the earth. He wrote, "Learn always to discriminate between things that differ. . . . Many run after novelties, charmed with every new thing; learn to judge between truth and its counterfeits, and you will not be led astray."[16]

Spurgeon was wary of any "new theology" that he thought contradicted the Holy Scriptures:

> There is a more dangerous spirit now abroad, entering into Non-
> conformist pulpits, and notably preventing the testimony of some
> . . . by those who reckon themselves to be men of culture and intel-
> lect. . . . Their theology is fickle as the wind. Landmarks are laughed
> at, and fixed teaching is despised. "Progress" is the watchword, and
> we hear it repeated *ad nauseum*. . . . It is often progress *from* the
> truth, which being interpreted, is progressing backwards.[17]

The clarion call of the Christian leader is to teach eternal truths to his followers. "Go over the fundamental truths with your hearers very carefully.
. . . Make them know the first principles of the faith. It will not weary your

hearers, it will bless them, and many of them will be delighted. Repeat the fundamentals, too; often, if you can."[18]

Grounded in Biblical Doctrine

The Christian leader must be resolute in his commitment to the full redemptive revelation of God through the Holy Scriptures. Spurgeon attributed all of his theological beliefs to the teachings of the Bible, according to his comprehension of its truths. He was a biblicist at heart and did not entertain any theological speculations that were inconsistent with the Word of God. In Eric Hayden's book *Letting the Lion Loose: C. H. Spurgeon and the Bible,* he compared Spurgeon to the eminent Puritan John Bunyan: "Prick him anywhere and he bleeds the Bible."[19]

Spurgeon credited much of his success to the fact that he was consistent in his interpretation of the Scriptures. In every facet of his ministry whether it was teaching, preaching, writing, counseling, or getting involved in public affairs he used the Bible. He counseled his students, "You must preach the whole of the gospel. The omission of a doctrine, or an ordinance, or a precept, may prove highly injurious."[20]

Biblical Authority

Spurgeon believed in the holy inspiration of the Bible. He wrote in his church newspaper, *The Sword and the Trowel,* that "the Holy Scriptures were written by inspiration, and are an infallible statement of truth . . . a doctrine about which we, at least, have no difficulty."[21] This was in contraposition to a number of evangelicals who were dabbling with other approaches to the Scriptures. Hayden, a twentieth-century pastor of the Metropolitan Tabernacle, writes concerning Spurgeon and the Bible,

> For Spurgeon . . . the Word of God was divinely inspired, authoritative, practical and comprehensive. Like the Puritans he believed the sacred book was sufficient for all faith and conduct. The Bible determined doctrine, worship, church order and government, and in private affected the Christian's life at home and away, at work and at play, his dress and his daily duty. The whole of his life was to be seen by the light of God's Word, the believer's "lamp for his feet and light for his path."[22]

As a leading dignitary of the Church of England aptly puts it, "Charles Haddon Spurgeon made the people feel that the Bible was a book never to be suspected, not to be apologized for, but a book to be believed and trusted, and received as the very Word of God."[23]

A Christian leader today who adheres to the authority of the Bible will meet definite challenges along the way. Barna, in *What Americans Believe,* reported that only 47 percent of all adult Americans strongly agree with the statement "The Bible is the written word of God and is totally accurate in all it teaches" (24 percent agree somewhat, 15 percent somewhat disagree, and 11 percent disagree strongly).[24] The framework of evangelical convictions is God's Word. It is our source of authority, and we must value it for what it is.

Spurgeon showed his undying loyalty to the revelation of Holy Scripture by his opposition to the new challenges of Darwinism, popularized by the publication of *The Origin of Species.* On one particular occasion, Spurgeon had a stuffed ape brought to the Tabernacle, whereupon he lectured on the theory of evolution and lampooned the errors of its hypotheses.

The Temptation to Compromise Convictions

Twenty-first-century Christian leaders are under increasing pressure to compromise their doctrinal convictions. Many reasons abound for such compromises, but among them is the practical demand and high expectations of churches for growth and prosperity. Pastors feel the real pressure to see visible growth in their church attendance, in their church buildings, and in their operating budgets. This underlying pressure to succeed can create an unhealthful environment that causes some leaders to go overboard in using questionable methods to enlarge their congregations. They can become obsessed with being "seeker driven" and "user friendly" to reach more people. In the process, they might risk watering down the gospel in an effort to reach their goals.

Pastors must be conscious of the danger of seeking so much to connect and identify with their hearers that they compromise the essence of the gospel. Os Guinness, in his caustic book *Dining with the Devil,* warned of the danger of frittering away the integrity of the gospel:

> But Scripture and history are clear: without maintaining critical
> tension, the principle of identification is a recipe for compromise
> and capitulation. It is no accident that the charge of being "all things

to all people" has become a popular synonym for compromise. If the process of becoming "all things to all people" is to remain faithful to Christ, it has to climax in clear persuasion and profound conversion. Joining people where they are is only the first step in the process, not the last. Unless it resists this danger, the megachurch and church-growth movement will prove to be a gigantic exercise in cultural adjustment and surrender.[25]

Leaders must not be driven by "growth pragmatism." Pastors must not divorce growth principles from Scripture. Such principles must be supportive of and not contradictory to biblical revelation.

Of course, on the other hand, the danger of dead orthodoxy always exists. Who wants to be "dead right," maintaining a watchful vigil over a lifeless congregation? Pastors must employ a sound theology, coupled with a passionate spirituality, to achieve the right balance. This is based on the conviction that the gospel message never changes whereas some methods of presenting and relating it may change. The methods must, however, be consistent with the claims of God's Word. Gene Mims warned, "Putting methods before the God-given process of church growth will endanger a church's long-term efforts to grow."[26]

A balance of biblical theology and godly inspiration will assure the Christian leader who seeks growth to be faithful to his calling. Spurgeon was all for growth and progress as long as it was the right kind of progress: "Is there to be no progress? Yes, within the lines of revealed truth; but there must be no departure from fixed principles."[27]

Standing for Righteousness

Spurgeon believed that standing for righteousness was a necessary validation of the effectiveness of one's ministry. He wrote, "Stand fast in the faith once for all delivered to the saints, and let no man spoil you by philosophy and vain deceit."[28] Spurgeon was ever inspired by the example of Christ. As Jesus gave Himself completely and became obedient, even to death on the Cross, His atoning sacrifice secured the salvation of those followers who receive eternal life through Him. Spurgeon believed that the minister, the Christian leader, must be an example of Christ, taking stands for righteousness that honor Christ. He said, "As He stood in our stead, *we also stand in His stead*. . . . For Him we stand in the pulpit, and speak of sin, and righteousness, and judgment to come."[29]

Facing the Real Enemy

The pastor of the Metropolitan Tabernacle recognized that the real enemy is not other Christians, unbelievers, or even oneself. He was convinced of the real existence of "this arch-enemy," Satan, and his influence in the world. He knew the truth of Ephesians 6:12: "For we do not wrestle against flesh and blood, but against principalities, against powers, against the rulers of the darkness of this age, against spiritual hosts of wickedness in the heavenly places" (NKJV). He counseled other ministers to persist in the face of difficulty: "The times are bad, but they have been bad before. You have to fight with Apollyon, but many met this arch-enemy before your day. Gird up the loins of your mind, and stand fast, for the Lord is greater than the times."[30]

Leaders today are involved in a spiritual battle as well. The ruler of this age seeks to gain the upper hand as Christians are confronted with issues such as abortion, alternative lifestyles, gay rights, substance abuse, sexual addiction, and family dysfunctions, to name a few. Christian leaders who seek to stand for righteousness will face opposition. Wherever God is at work, strongholds of resistance will be present. But the Scriptures give comfort to the leader who recognizes that the battle is the Lord's. Second Corinthians 10:4–5 reads, "For the weapons of our warfare are not carnal but mighty in God for pulling down strongholds, casting down arguments and every high thing that exalts itself against the knowledge of God, bringing every thought into captivity to the obedience of Christ" (NKJV).

Facing strongholds in opposition to the work of Christ requires great strength. Spurgeon believed that men who were prepared spiritually and operated out of firm convictions might not always win the day, but they would ultimately win the war. He called for ministers whose very lives were staked on truth and righteousness: "The want of the period is brethren who know the gospel for themselves, who have had a personal experience of its power, who have tested it as silver is tried in a furnace of earth, and who set such a value upon it, that they would sooner part with life than give it up."[31]

Christian leaders today can take heart in the inspiring example set by C. H. Spurgeon more than a hundred years ago. The cause of righteousness is no less important now than it was then. The battle is the same one he fought, and each leader must consider whether he is up to the challenge. Spurgeon believed that Christians are different, distinctive from the world. The world is going one direction, but believers are going in another direction. Those people with the courage of conviction will stand strong in the power of Christ.

> You see that the men of this world are coming this way in a great crowd, all in a hurry, rushing after their gods. And we believers, what are we doing? Threading our way, as best we can, pushing our way "against" the stream, going in an exactly opposite direction to the rest of mankind.
>
> Some of you cannot do this—you keep getting carried off your legs, and you are swept along by the torrent. But the man of God must go against the current. He is not to be swept back—but he is always pressing forward, ever seeking to make an advance, contending for every inch, and making up his mind that, come what may, he cannot go back. That is not his way—he must go forward, ever pressing on toward the city that has foundations.[32]

SPURGEON'S LEADERSHIP LESSONS

- **A true leader is willing to stand by the courage of his convictions.**
  When it came to leadership issues related to sin and righteousness,
  Spurgeon yielded no ground whatsoever. If he encountered error, he
  would confront it. "We must not allow sin to go unrebuked. Yield in all
  things personal, but be firm where truth and holiness are concerned."
- **People are inspired when their leaders show the willingness to risk
  everything for their beliefs.** Billy Graham testified, "Courage is contagious." The congregation at the Metropolitan Tabernacle was bolstered
  by the courageous stands that their pastor took in his advocacy of the
  gospel.
- **A leader is resolute when it comes to matters of spirituality and
  Christian conduct.** Because he was confident in his doctrinal beliefs
  and firmly grounded in the Scriptures, Spurgeon was willing to stand
  alone if necessary when it came to the cause of righteousness.
- **A leader must seek the wisdom and discernment that comes from
  God in confronting error.** A leader faces many challenges to his beliefs
  along the way and must discover for which ones he is willing to fight.
  Spurgeon wrote, "Learn always to discriminate between things that differ; . . . Learn to judge between truth and counterfeits, and you will not be
  led astray."
- **Principled confidence comes to the leader who is well grounded in
  his theological beliefs.** Spurgeon's system of belief was based on evangelical Calvinism, which he modified only to the extent that he was able
  to make a broader appeal in the presentation of the gospel.
- **Complacency cannot be condoned when it comes to a leader's theological knowledge.** Spurgeon believed that many errors could be avoided
  if one became competent and equipped in his or her theology. "Be well
  instructed in theology, and do not regard . . . those who rail at it because
  they are ignorant of it."
- **The Christian leader must be firmly resolute in his commitment to
  the full redemptive revelation of God through the Holy Scriptures.**
  "You must preach the whole of the gospel. The omission of a doctrine, or
  an ordinance, or a precept, may prove highly injurious."
- **Standing for righteousness is a necessary validation of the effectiveness of one's ministry.** Spurgeon wrote, "Stand fast in the faith
  once for all delivered to the saints, and let no man spoil you by philosophy and vain deceit."

- **It takes great strength to face strongholds in opposition to the work of Christ.** Spurgeon believed that men who are prepared spiritually and operate out of firm convictions might not always win the day, but they will ultimately win the war.

8

COMMITMENT

Teaching and Modeling Devotion to Family

We ought to be such husbands that every husband in the parish may safely be such as we are. Is it so? We ought to be the best of fathers. Alas! some ministers, to my knowledge, are far from this, for as to their families, they have kept the vineyards of others, but their own vineyards they have not kept.[1]

One standard by which you can measure the quality of a leader is the level of priority he gives to his family. A Christian leader understands that one of the primary ways to honor God is by honoring one's family.

C. H. Spurgeon testified that his allegiance to his own family was due to the fact that he was blessed to be born into a Christian family—what he referred to as a "goodly heritage."[2] Spurgeon not only realized the benefits of his own heritage but also considered it his God-given responsibility to pass those blessings on to his own wife and children. Spurgeon's devotion to his family was a characteristic that complemented his service to God.

Leaders today have no less pressure to demonstrate that they have good family relationships. The challenge is to have the same dedication to one's family as to one's ministry/vocation. Some leaders are prone to devote themselves endlessly to their careers and vocations, often to the neglect of their spouses and families. Countless stories abound regarding self-serving leaders who have sacrificed their families on the altar of ministry success.

The Price of Success

Marilee Pierce Dunker, daughter of the founder of World Vision, Bob Pierce, writes about her father's choice of his international ministry over his family in her book *Days of Glory, Seasons of Night*. Affectionately but honestly, she shares how her father confused his commitments to his ministry with his obligations at home. It was a tough choice for Pierce, who was experiencing tremendous success as thousands of people came to Christ through his mission preaching overseas. In the course of his growing ministry, however, Pierce neglected his family, often being gone for as long as ten months at a time. It eventually cost him his marriage, one of his three daughters committed suicide, and Pierce died alone. Although some people might consider his singular commitment to his ministry as heroic dedication, the casualties of his family relationships revealed a lack of devotion to the closest ones committed to his care. Pierce is an example of what can happen when a leader, if he is careless, becomes so engrossed in his own personal calling that he fails in his ministry to his own family.

Spurgeon saw similar patterns among the ministerial leadership in his day. He was chagrined over the attitudes of some of his peers, who were selfishly enslaved to their own egos:

> For them, their wives exist; for them, their children are born; for them, everything is placed where it appears in God's universe; and they judge all things according to this one rule, "How will it benefit me?" That is the beginning and the end of their grand system, and they expect the daily revolution, if not of all the heavenly bodies, certainly of all the earthly bodies around them.
>
> The sun, the moon, and the eleven stars are to make obeisance to them. Well, brethren, that is an exploded theory so far as the earth is concerned, and there is no truth in such a notion with reference to ourselves. We may cherish the erroneous idea; but the general public will not, and the sooner the grace of God expels it from us, the better, so that we may take our proper position in a far higher system than any of which we can ever be the center.[3]

Spurgeon knew that there are always a certain group of leaders who believe themselves to be the center of the universe. In their system of self-exaltation, everything else, including family, exists only to please them. Their wives and children are placed in their home to suit their own whims and for their own convenience. Everything revolves around the self-centeredness of such leaders. Unfortunately, this characteristic is as prevalent today among some Christian leaders as it is among non-Christian leaders. It is not rare to see a well-known leader fall because of self-centered pursuits that compromise his or her ministry. Occasionally, given the arrogance and smugness of certain so-called Christian leaders, one wonders whose kingdom they are seeking to build.

The Priority of Family

The Christian leader's first priority is not himself; his primary commitment is to Christ. He must lay himself on the altar before God and deny himself in following Christ. His next priority is to the persons whom God has placed under his roof. He has a unique role in providing godly leadership to the people closest to him—his own family. Yes, many demands outside the home are placed on a leader, but he has to make a choice. The right choice is to prioritize his commitment to his family. God has placed him as the head of his home, and he must assume that spiritual responsibility and the practical functions of it.

In his book *Rediscovering the Soul of Leadership,* Eugene Habecker prescribes the following antidotes for leaders who are concerned about their relationship with their spouse and families: take regular vacations, do something special, make spiritual renewal as a couple a continuous journey, share your worlds, and share family financial information.[4] Although these antidotes do not provide a total picture of what comprises a healthy family, they offer positive direction for any leader who is seeking guidance in matters of family priorities. More than anything else, family members want to know that they are a special priority in their spouse's or parents' life.

Unfortunately, many current books on Christian leadership offer little counsel regarding specific ways a leader should relate to his family. What seems to be omitted or assumed is the essential role that a leader has in his home. The manner in which a man leads in his home has direct implications on how he will lead in his work. If he succeeds at home first, that success will undergird his work at the office or on the job. If he fails with his family, he ultimately will fail in his all-encompassing role as a leader. All of the success in the world cannot replace what a leader loses when he fails in the primary responsibility of leading his family.

Receiving a Godly Heritage

A godly heritage is great gain for the Christian leader. The one who has benefited from the influence of Christian upbringing in the home has a great advantage in providing the right kind of leadership to his own family.

Spurgeon's parents and grandparents instilled in him Christian virtues and a love for the things of God. He was born in 1834, the firstborn child of John and Eliza Spurgeon. Both his father and his grandfather were Congregationalist pastors. When he was a young boy, extenuating circumstances and economic hardships created the need for him to live for several years at his grandparents' home at Stambourne, the necessity of which proved to be an act of providence.

Young Spurgeon lived with his grandparents during most of his first five years and then spent many summers with them for the rest of his childhood. There, under the tutelage of his Puritan grandfather, James Spurgeon, young Charles was steeped in the teachings of the Puritans. It began with an introduction to *Pilgrim's Progress* and continued with other great works. His grandparents doted upon him, disciplined him, loved him, and mentored him in the ways of God. At an early age, he was allowed to read the Scriptures at family prayer and often stopped to ask his grandfather questions about difficult passages. Spurgeon recounted the horror that he felt when his grandfather gave his interpretation of "the bottomless pit":

> There is a deep pit, and the soul is falling down—oh, how fast it is falling! There! the last ray of light at the top has disappeared, and it falls on—on—on, and so it goes on falling—on—on—on for a thousand years! . . . The soul goes on falling perpetually into a deeper depth still, falling for ever into . . . the pit that has no bottom! Woe, without termination, without hope of its coming to a conclusion![5]

His grandfather's vivid rendering of hell made upon the young boy's receptive mind an indelible impression of the horror of sin and its eternal consequences.

A Succession of Family Ministers

His spiritual heritage was of great importance to young Charles. He took pride in the fact that he was in a lengthy line of ministers, some of whom had experienced hardship and persecution for their faith. He boasted, "I had far rather be descended from one who suffered for the faith than bear the blood of all the emperors within my veins."[6] Although some evidence exists that he descended from some of the heroic Norsemen, Spurgeon was more proud of the fact that his forefathers included Protestants who had fled Catholic persecution in Europe in the seventeenth century and sought refuge in England. Among them was a Job Spurgeon, who was imprisoned a number of times because of his Nonconformist convictions. Spurgeon identified with his ancestor:

> In my seasons of suffering, I have often pictured to myself this modern Job in Chelmsford gaol, and thanked God that I bore the same name as this persecuted Spurgeon of two hundred years ago. . . . I sometimes feel the shadow of his broad brim come over my spirit. Grace is not tied to families, but yet the Lord delights to bless to a thousand generations. There is a sweet fitness in the passing on of holy loyalty from grandsire to father, and from father to son.[7]

The future of young Charles and his great influence as a minister of the gospel was prophesied when a famous preacher named Richard Knill visited Stambourne on a certain occasion. He spent a great deal of time with Charles and pronounced that the young boy would grow up to preach the gospel to the largest congregations in the world. His prophecy later was fulfilled as Spurgeon followed the calling that led to great renown as a minister of the gospel. Like pastors today who have the advantage of a godly heritage, Spurgeon was fortunate that he was given a firm foundation in the ways of the Lord that served him well the rest of his life.

The Leader as a Family Model

Spurgeon believed that one of the reasons many working men did not follow their pastor's leadership at church was because they did not believe them to be "real men." He encouraged pastors to be men who demonstrated their humanity in a manly fashion:

> I am persuaded that one reason why our working-men so universally keep clear of ministers is because they abhor their artificial and unmanly ways. If they saw us, in the pulpit and out of it, acting

like real men, and speaking naturally, like honest men, they would
come around us. . . . We must have humanity along with our divinity if we would win the masses. Everybody can see through affecta-
tions, and people are not likely to be taken in by them.[8]

Spurgeon was addressing the effeminate way in which many ministers
came across to the average working man. The frail clergy offered from the
pulpit pious platitudes and syrupy language that did not connect with the
man on the street. They seldom spoke honestly to real issues that working
men and their families faced. At the same time, Spurgeon believed that parishioners were looking for a godly male example in both the pulpit and the
home. That leader should be the same person at home as he is with the public. Often, the public image and the private persona are two different people.
Spurgeon warned those who thought that they could neglect their private
conduct at home, "It is not sufficient for us to maintain our public reputation among our fellow-creatures, for our God can see in the wall, he notices
our coldness in the closet of communion, and he perceives our faults and
failures in the family."[9]

C. H. Spurgeon was a consistent Christian model to his family, as he was to
his church and the other people who subscribed to his ministries. But he never
regarded it as an easy task,

> Do you find it easy, my brethren, to be saints?—such saints that
> others may regard you as examples? We ought to be such husbands
> that every husband in the parish may safely be such as we are. Is it
> so? We ought to be the best of fathers. Alas! some ministers, to my
> knowledge, are far from this, for as to their families, they have kept
> the vineyards of others, but their own vineyards they have not kept.
> Their children are neglected, and do not grow up as a godly seed. Is
> it so with yours? In our converse with our fellow men are we blame-
> less and harmless, the sons of God without rebuke? Such we ought
> to be.[10]

The Model of Devotion and Prayer

The leader should set the example of devotion and prayer in the home. A
close friend of Spurgeon's commented on his prayer life, "His public prayers

were an inspiration, but his prayers with the family were to me more wonderful still. Mr. Spurgeon, when bowed before God in family prayer, appeared a grander man even than when holding thousands spellbound by his oratory."[11] Mrs. Spurgeon remembered,

> At the tea-table, the conversation was bright, witty, and always interesting; and after the meal was over, an adjournment was made to the study for family worship, and it was at these seasons that my beloved's prayers were remarkable for their tender childlikeness, their spiritual pathos, and their intense devotion. He seemed to come as near to God as a little child to a loving father, and we were often moved to tears as he talked thus face to face with his Lord.[12]

Spurgeon told pastors how one should set the example: "He prays as a husband and as a father; he strives to make his family devotions a model for his flock."[13] Many leaders today have gotten away from family devotions at home, but that quality time with family around God's Word is essential for the one who seeks to lead his family in spiritual matters.

A Christian leader should seek to lead his children to faith in Christ. Spurgeon lamented the neglect of fathers to lead their children in the most important matter of life. He shared the following instance of the terrible consequence that came to a father who did not take his role seriously:

> I have heard of some persons who have had objections to labor for the conversion of their children on the ground that God would save his own without any effort on our part. I remember making one man wince who held this view, by telling him of a father who would never teach his child to pray, or have him instructed even as to the meaning of prayer. He thought it was wrong, and that such work ought to be left to God's Holy Spirit. The boy fell down, and broke his leg, and had to have it taken off; and all the while the surgeon was amputating it, the boy was cursing and swearing in the most frightful manner. The good surgeon said to the father, "You see, you would not teach your boy to pray, but the Devil evidently had no objection to teach him to swear." That is the mischief of it; if we do not try our best to bring our children to Christ, there is another who will do his worst to drag them down to hell.[14]

On the other hand, Spurgeon rejoiced to see the fruit of his spiritual labors with his own children. He recounted the conversion of his twin sons:

> Did not our hearts overflow, as parents, when we first discovered that our children had sought the Lord? That was a happy night, a time to be remembered, when we were called up to hear their tearful story, and to give them a word of comfort. We were not half so glad at their birth as we were when they were born again. Have we not, since then, often rejoiced as we have seen them useful in the service of the Savior? It was an exquisite pleasure to hear them speak for the first time in the Redeemer's Name; and it has been a greater pleasure to know that God has owned their ministry in the conversion of souls. All parents have not that particular form of joy; but it has been mine to a high degree, and for this I bless the Name of the Lord. All of you have had great delight in your converted children, when your boy has stood out against temptation, or your girl has remained faithful when thrown among worldlings. No one can recount the mutual joys of the various members of a believing household; they rejoice in each other, and then, they all rejoice in God. How cheering it is for you as a parent to live again in your children, and to march once more to the holy war in the vigorous zeal of one whom you still call "My boy!" O friends, I feel, at this time, in my own case, that my joy is up to the brim of my life-cup. Pardon me if I pause to magnify the Lord. I have seldom been long without affliction; but no man who has ever lived could have been more highly favored in domestic happiness than I have been.[15]

Nothing gave the acclaimed pastor more joy than to see his own sons follow in his footsteps by their faith in Christ.

Mentoring Children in the Faith

A Christian leader seeks to mentor his children in the faith. Spurgeon sought to do just that with his twin sons, Thomas and Charles. Spurgeon was extremely fond of his sons and developed a loving relationship with them. Family devotions were conducted regularly, as reflected in the comments of Thomas:

"Family worship was a delightful item of each day's doings."[16] Spurgeon normally conducted the devotions, and Thomas remarked that "his unstudied comments, and his marvelous prayers, were an inspiration indeed."[17]

Spurgeon often took the boys for outings when the weather and his health allowed. They would venture into the scenic English valleys, taking long walks and enjoying a packed lunch together. Thomas remembered, "We lunched beneath the fir trees, where meanwhile the birds were singing to us. No wonder, then, that the poetic fire burst forth, and C.H.S. gave vent to his delight in extempore rhyme."[18]

Occasionally, the boys accompanied Spurgeon to the European continent, where they sometimes assisted in hosting others who joined them on the trips. They enjoyed the conversations and exchanges that their father had with guests at their hotels, and they learned from their father's ability to discourse with so many different types of people.

Both Thomas and Charles received the calling to vocational ministry and became pastors. Charles remained in London for the duration of his ministry. Thomas, however, became the more notable of the two sons. Upon recognition of his pastoral gifts, he received a calling to go far away from home, to Australia and New Zealand, where he ministered effectively for a number of years. Thomas returned to London in 1894, after his father's death, to succeed his father as the pastor of the Metropolitan Tabernacle. As it is for the children of many famous parents, it was difficult for Thomas to follow in his father's footsteps and live up to the high expectations that were placed upon him. His ministry was a faithful one, but it never rivaled the acclaim of his father.

Positive Influence Toward God

Leaders have a great responsibility when it comes to their children. Eugene Habecker encourages leaders to do the following regarding their children: be flexible, find common interests, keep home and office separate, emphasize the positive aspects of leadership, and plan for the long term.[19] Spurgeon's perspective included patience: "True fathers are patient; they do not expect to find old heads on young shoulders. They have the knack of waiting till tomorrow, for time brings with it many instructions."[20]

In *An All-Round Ministry,* Spurgeon warned Christian leaders of the responsibility that accompanies the role of father. "The parental relation is one which requires much of us." He went on to counsel leaders to enact the role of father in their ministries: "A father should be a stable and established man; the spiritual father is full of tenderness; the father of a family usually finds that his pre-eminence is one of superior self-denial, rather than of self-assertion; a father must possess wisdom; he must know the weighty responsibility of a father towards his children."[21]

Spurgeon demonstrated the type of love that he had for his sons in a letter that he wrote to "Charlie" as his son was about to leave school and embark on a career:

> . . . I am full of hope about you; and if I feel any anxiety, it is because I love you so well that I want you to be a greater success than other young men. I believe you love the Lord, and that is the main thing; the next is, stick *to it.*
>
> Leave childish things once for all, and buckle to the work. It will not be pleasant, and it may even become irksome; but the harder you work, at first, the less you will have to do in later life. The times are so pushing that you must put out all your energies; and, above all, you must be careful, and very persevering; and then, with God's blessing, you will soon take a position to which your father and mother can point with pleasure.[22]

He encouraged his sons in their ministerial calling and commended their efforts, as seen in the following note to Charles:

> My Dear Son—Your note was a real joy to me. What a good fellow you are! I live twice in seeing you so firm in the faith of God's elect. I do not wonder that the chickens flock around the man who gives them real corn, and not mere chaff. The Lord keep you evermore true to the truth, and you will see His hand with you more and more! Your little notices of books are first-rate; short and pithy, better than half a page of long-winded nothings. You may do as many as ever you like, for nobody can do them better, nor as well.[23]

Both Thomas and Charles adored their father and sought to please him through their ministerial offices. Great joy comes to the leader who lives to see his children follow in his footsteps. No greater pleasure comes than seeing that one's life and ministry have made that kind of impression and impact upon one's own children. It is certainly one of the greatest blessings on earth.

Sharing Ministry with Family

A leader who shares his leadership responsibilities with family members can receive a tremendous blessing. Spurgeon's brother James became an integral part of his ministry as an associate pastor, relieving his brother of many of the pastoral burdens that could be safely entrusted to him.

James Archer Spurgeon became Charles's associate pastor at the Metropolitan Tabernacle in 1868, and he remained in that position until the pastor's death in 1892. James served in this capacity while at the same time serving as pastor in another church in London. He became an invaluable asset to his more famous brother, their relationship being one of strong affection and loyalty.

Actually, James became the administrator of many of the pastoral ministries that his brother had delegated to him. Charles was in charge, but James provided the loyalty and consistency of ministry that afforded his brother the opportunity to travel, preach, and be away for long periods of recuperation during and following times of illness. In offering James the position, the elders wrote to him,

> We ask your aid mainly in pastoral work, in visiting the sick, in seeing inquirers, in attending at church-meetings, and in such other works as naturally fall to the lot of a Pastor. Your brother has many great works in hand, and you have already so efficiently aided him in our College, and in the Orphanage, that we are sure that you will in all other things afford him such brotherly assistance as he may from time to time require. Our earnest prayer is that to us you may be a great blessing, leading on the entire church, both by your example and precept, in the path of earnest labor for the Lord, who has redeemed us by His most precious blood.[24]

During one of Spurgeon's absences due to illness, his church officers wrote to him, assuring him of the contribution of his brother's ministry:

> Our Co-pastor, your beloved brother, is laboring among us, during your absence, with indefatigable zeal and increasing success. He is daily growing in our affection and esteem; and we bless God for providing you with such a faithful coadjutor in the work He has given you to do.[25]

During the Downgrade Controversy, James happened to be a member of the Council of the Baptist Union, with whom Spurgeon was in disagreement. James seemed unable to see the ramifications of some of the official actions taken by the Baptist Union regarding his brother. At the climax of the controversy at the annual assembly of the Baptist Union, James seconded a motion regarding his brother and the conflict at hand. Unfortunately, Charles interpreted the near-unanimous affirmative vote as a personal censure. However, he held no malice toward his brother James for his involvement in the unfortunate turn of events, and their relationship remained strong throughout those turbulent times.

James became interim pastor of the Metropolitan Tabernacle after his brother's death and remained such until his nephew was called as the pastor two years later. Spurgeon testified of his brother's ministry and teaching in one of his annual addresses to The Pastors' College:

> I adore the goodness of God which sent me so dear and efficient a fellow-helper as my brother in the flesh and in the Lord, J. A. Spurgeon. His work has greatly relieved me of anxiety, and his superior educational qualifications have tended to raise the tone of the instruction given.[26]

Blessed is the leader who is able to share the responsibilities of ministry with capable and trustworthy family associates.

Joint Ministry with Spouse

Christian leaders who partner with their spouses can attain mutual fulfillment through joint ventures in ministry. Spurgeon's wife Susannah, although unwell for much of her adult life, initiated ministries that not only gave her much personal fulfillment but also complemented the pastoral ministry of her husband. That fact should be expected when one comprehends that Susannah Spurgeon was the love of Charles's life. He often wrote of his love for her:

> Think of the love which gave me that dear lady for a wife, and made her such a wife; to me, the ideal wife, and, as I believe, without exaggeration or love-flourishing, the precise form in which God

would make a woman for such a man as I am, if He designed her to be the greatest of all earthly blessings to him.[27]

They met during the first year of his ministry in London. Susannah was converted under his preaching, and Charles baptized her. Shortly thereafter, they were married. Thus began a life of sweet devotion and marital fidelity that lasted throughout their lives. Spurgeon reflected on the blessing of the quality of relationship between them:

> Matrimony came from Paradise, and leads to it. I never was half so happy, before I was a married man, as I am now. When you are married, your bliss begins. Let the husband love his wife as he loves himself, and a little better, for she is his better half. He should feel, *"If* there's only one good wife in the whole world, I've got her."[28]

Pastors' wives have a difficult task, and it was even more so for the wife of the pastor of the Metropolitan Tabernacle. Spurgeon described the difficulties and privileges of a pastor's wife on the occasion of his son's wedding:

> If I was a young woman, and was thinking of being married, I would not marry a minister, because the position of minister's wife is a very difficult one for anyone to fill. Churches do not give a married minister two salaries, one for the husband and the other for the wife; but, in many cases, they look for the services of the wife, whether they pay for them or not. The Pastor's wife is expected to know everything about the church, and in another sense she is to know nothing of it; and she is equally blamed by some people whether she knows everything or nothing. Her duties consist in being *always at home* to attend to her husband and her family, and being *always out,* visiting other people, and doing all sorts of things for the whole church! Well, of course, that is impossible; she cannot be at everybody's beck and call, and she cannot expect to please everybody. . . . Difficulties arise continually in the best-regulated churches; and the position of the minister's wife is always a very trying one. Still, I think that, if I was a Christian young woman, I would marry a Christian minister if I could, because there is an opportunity of doing so much good in helping him in his service

for Christ. It is a great assistance to the cause of God to keep the
minister himself in good order for his work. It is his wife's duty to
see that he is not uncomfortable at home; for, if everything there is
happy, and free from care, he can give all his thoughts to his
preparation for the pulpit; and the godly woman, who thus helps
her husband to preach better, is herself a preacher though she never
speaks in public, and she becomes to the highest degree useful to
that portion of the Church of Christ which is committed to her
husband's charge.[29]

Susannah Spurgeon's Partnership

Susannah Spurgeon was a great emotional support to her husband throughout their marriage and, in many ways, was the ideal pastor's wife. She devoted
much of her time to her husband's ministry. She collected all of Spurgeon's
news clippings and articles into scrapbooks, which gave a complete account of
Spurgeon's many activities during his illustrious ministry.

Spurgeon traveled a great deal, which meant that he often was away from
his young wife. She would pace the floor at night, praying for his safe return,
and was always so relieved and overjoyed when she heard him at the door. On
one occasion, she broke down in tears because of a distant engagement that
Spurgeon had to fulfill. The young pastor reminded her of the Israelites offering their lambs to God at the altar and that the sacrifice was a time of rejoicing, not sadness. He posed a question to her: "You are giving me to God in
letting me go to preach the Gospel to poor sinners, and do you think he likes
to see you cry over the sacrifice?" Susie, as he affectionately called her, pon-
dered his words and later remarked, "It sank deep into my heart, carrying comfort; and thence-forward when I parted with him, the tears were scarcely ever
allowed to show themselves."[30] If a stray one came forth, Spurgeon would say,
"What! Crying over your lamb, Wifey!" And his reminder quickly dried her
tears and put a smile in their place.

Challenging Health Issues

Spurgeon's wife suffered from various illnesses throughout her life and was
often confined to home with her ailments. Regardless of her own physical restrictions, however, she continued the work on her scrapbook and her active

prayer life for the ministry of the church. Although Spurgeon was away many times, he was at her side as often as he could be.

> My beloved husband, always so fully engaged about his Master's business, yet managed to secure many precious moments by my side; when he would tell me how the work of the Lord was prospering in his hands, and we would exchange sympathies, he comforting me in my suffering, and I cheering him on in his labor.[31]

Many times when Spurgeon went to Mentone to recover from his extended bouts with rheumatic gout, Susannah had to stay behind in London. They wrote to each other extensively and kept their communications most active during those times of separation.

Susannah might not have been a hearty soul when it came to personal health, but she refused to let it overcome her life. She prayed for some vital role that she could play in her husband's all-encompassing ministry. She felt led of the Lord to establish a ministry called the Book Fund that blessed many pastors and laypeople. It began with a challenge upon the publication of Spurgeon's *Lectures to My Students* in 1875 to place that volume in the hands of every minister in England. Taking all of the money that she had saved for such a special idea, she established the Book Fund. Through additional donations and contributions, the fund grew, and, as a result, many poor ministers were provided with Christian books that furthered the effectiveness of their ministries. Also, she started the Colportage Association, which delivered books and resources to ministers in rural parts of the country.

Like all other couples, the Spurgeons undoubtedly had times of disagreement within their home. But such was their tremendous love for and commitment to each other that they provided a shining example to other couples in their church and community.

Father to the Fatherless

Spurgeon was a father figure to many of his parishioners at the Metropolitan Tabernacle. Because many of them had come to faith under his ministry, he considered his role to be that of a spiritual father to them.

The kinship that Spurgeon felt for family was evident in his desire to be a "father to the fatherless." Because London and surrounding areas had so many orphaned children, the need for a home for them was abundant. Spurgeon had been inspired by the orphanage work of George Müller in Bristol, and he put the challenge to his people at the Metropolitan Tabernacle. Through the initial gift of a large sum of money from a lady in his church, the vision for an orphanage became a reality. Because Spurgeon was convinced that children needed families, he constructed the facility so that children were not placed in large workrooms together; rather, each child was placed in a family unit with a Christian "mother" assigned to each unit.

> Children need something more than a roof and four walls to shelter them; they want a home where the virtues of a Christian character shall be fostered and developed. When an institution is adapted as far as possible to compensate the loss of parental influence and control, one essential element of success is secured.[32]

Christmas at the Orphanage

The Stockwell Orphanage became the institution whereby Spurgeon became a surrogate father for many homeless children. Every Christmas, with few exceptions, he spent the day at the orphanage, where the joy of his extended family brought great blessing to his life and theirs. To this day, the influence of Spurgeon upon homeless children continues, because thousands of orphans have come through that institution to become productive Christians and citizens.

Spurgeon also extended his fathering to the students at The Pastors' College. In the preface of one of his books, the editor wrote about the annual conference, at which Spurgeon always gave the President's Address:

> MR. SPURGEON always regarded the Conference week as one of the most important in the whole year; and he devoted much time, and thought, and care, and prayer, to the preparation of his Addresses to the hundreds of ministers and students who then gathered together from all parts of the kingdom and from distant lands also. Surrounded by his sons in the faith, many of whom were his own spiritual children, and all of whom delighted to call him Presi-

dent, leader, brother, friend, he spoke with a freedom and a home-
liness which could never be excelled, nor hardly equaled, in any
other assembly; and the Addresses themselves supply abundant
evidence of the solemn responsibility which he felt in speaking to
such an audience, and of the faithfulness with which he discharged
that responsibility.[33]

C. H. Spurgeon saw the role of family leader as one that began at home and
then extended to other areas of ministry. He accomplished much because he
loved his parishioners, his students, and his orphans as though they were his
own dear family. He counseled other pastors, "Be to your people like a father
among his children, or an elder brother among his brethren, that you may
be the means of blessing to them, and at the same time meet the evil of
disintegration."[34]

In a day in which we see much disintegration of families, not only in secular
realms but also in the church, leaders must renew their commitment to their
own families. As they devote themselves to their own dear ones, God will enable them to extend that familial ministry beyond their own four walls at home.
Through example, commitment, discipline, and undying love, a leader can
broaden his influence to include many to whom he ministers as a shepherd in
the body of Christ.

SPURGEON'S LEADERSHIP LESSONS

- **The leader who prioritizes a commitment to his family honors the God whom he serves.** Spurgeon gave great attention and devotion to his family, as evidenced by their testimonies in his *Autobiography.* His wife and sons grew to love and serve the Lord under his influence.
- **A godly heritage is great gain for the Christian leader.** Spurgeon was blessed to have been born into and reared by a family that instilled in him Christian virtues and a love for the things of God.
- **A leader who shares his leadership with family can receive a tremendous blessing.** Spurgeon's brother James became an integral part of his ministry as an associate pastor, relieving his brother of many of the pastoral burdens that could be safely entrusted to him.
- **Christian pastors who partner with their spouses can enjoy ministry opportunities together.** Spurgeon's wife Susannah, although unwell for much of her adult life, initiated ministries that gave her much personal fulfillment and complemented the pastoral ministry of her husband.
- **A Christian leader seeks to mentor his children in the faith.** Spurgeon savored every opportunity to influence his sons for good, as is evident in an excerpt from a letter to Charles: "I am full of hope about you. . . . I believe you love the Lord, and that is the main thing; the next is, stick *to it.* . . . The times are so pushing that you must put out all your energies; and, above all, you must be careful, and very persevering; and then, with God's blessing, you will soon take a position to which your father and mother can point with pleasure."
- **A leader should be the same person at home that he is with the public.** "It is not sufficient for us to maintain our public reputation among our fellow-creatures, for our God . . . notices our coldness in the closet of communion, and he perceives our faults and failures in the family."
- **The leader should set the example of devotion and prayer in the home.** "He prays as a husband and as a father; he strives to make his family devotions a model for his flock. . . ."
- **Christian leaders should seek to lead their children to faith in Christ.** "If we do not try our best to bring our children to Christ, there is another who will do his worst to drag them down to hell."
- **A leader's fatherly influence extends beyond his home to those under his leadership.** "Be to your people like a father among his children . . . that you may be the means of blessing to them, and at the same time meet the evil of disintegration."

9

CREATIVITY

Preaching, Methods, and Ministry Innovations

I am not very scrupulous about the means I use for doing good.
. . . I would preach standing on my head, if I thought I could
convert your souls.[1]

A creative God calls creative leaders to engage in the creative enterprise of propagating His kingdom's work. The God who created the vast universe in which we live, with all of the intricacies and variations of His creation, is the same God who gifts leaders with spiritual gifts and creative abilities to provide leadership for each successive generation. We humans have creative ability because we are made in the image of our Creator. Creativity is working with, rather than against, the Creator. If we in the church are not careful, we might negate our creative potential and become predictable, dull, monotonous, and lethargic in our ministries. This prospect is a slap in the face to our incredible, ever-surprising, and infinite Creator, whose ways are beyond our finite comprehension and who is ever leading us forward to claim the promise: "Behold I make all things new."

Spurgeon believed that bold, creative faith is the defining difference for doing great things for God:

> Our faith makes us abundant in good works. May I say to you, if you are doing all you possibly can for Christ, endeavor to do yet more? I believe a Christian man is generally right when he is doing more than he can; and when he goes still further beyond that point, he will be even more nearly right. There are scarcely any bounds to the possibilities of our service. Many a man, who now is doing little,

might, with the same exertion, do twice as much by wise arrange-
ment and courageous enterprise. . . . We need, like the apostles, to
launch out into the deep, or our nets will never enclose a great
multitude of fishes. If we had but the pluck to come out of our
hiding-places, and face the foe, we should soon achieve immense
success. We need far more faith in the Holy Ghost. He will bless us
if we cast ourselves entirely upon Him.[2]

He contended that the one who accomplishes much is the leader who declares,
"I know whom I have believed, I know what I have experienced."[3] He is the
man who can run upon the Lord's errands.

In a day in which resources are plentiful and opportunities for improvement and training abound, we have no excuse not to be creative. Failure to do
so very well may be a sin. Far too many Christian leaders do not realize their
potential for creativity. They have accepted the routine, the status quo, the
inevitable rut that they have dug for themselves. They assume that they are not
able to do anything original, so they beg, borrow, and steal from others, believing the lie that others' work is better than their own. But, for many such
people, their efforts are to no avail. They seem to be uncreative, boring, pas-
sionless, unmotivated, and minimally interested in the most important mission of the universe—to communicate the gospel of Jesus Christ to an unsaved
world!

The gospel message does not change, but the manner of its presentation
may be adapted according to the situation required. Although a Christian leader
must be careful that he does not compromise the unchanging message of salvation through Christ alone, the means of communicating that message are as
varied as the people whom we seek to reach.

Personal Distinctions

C. H. Spurgeon had no familiarity with the idea of being uncreative in pursuing his ministerial calling—in fact, he was just the opposite. He used all of
the creative energies at his disposal to communicate the gospel to the thousands of people who came to hear him preach. Upon his arrival in London at
the age of nineteen, people noticed immediately that he was not like the typical preachers of the day. He didn't look like them, he didn't talk like them, he
didn't use the same mannerisms, and he didn't observe the same decorum.

The ministers of the Church of England, the predominant denomination in the city, dressed in ornate clerical robes. As a Baptist, Spurgeon preferred to wear a dark business suit. The Anglican clerics usually spoke in hushed and "reverent" tones. Spurgeon was loud, dramatic, and boisterous in his presentation. The typical clergy used stilted and predictable mannerisms; most of the preachers read in monotones from full manuscripts. Spurgeon took only sparse notes into the pulpit with him, and he preached extemporaneously.

Numerous pastors today use creative approaches in their effort to proclaim the gospel. They might incorporate drama, show brief video clips, or use PowerPoint presentations. A popular trend among some churches is to replace their solid wooden pulpit with a clear acrylic podium. They believe that the wooden pulpit is a barrier to communication, an object that comes between the speaker and the hearer. They believe that the clear pulpit, on the other hand, communicates openness with the hearers. If this view is true, perhaps Spurgeon was way ahead of his time. He used no pulpit whatsoever. In the Metropolitan Tabernacle, he preached from the second-level platform with a curved rostrum, which projected out from the front of the first gallery. It had an open railing, and contained a table and a settee for the pastor, behind which was a row of chairs for the deacons. Spurgeon used only the table at his side, upon which he placed his Bible. This setup gave him full and complete freedom to move about and use the space on the platform.

Shunning Tradition

In addition to abandoning the traditional pulpit, Spurgeon shunned other pastoral traditions of his day. He refused ordination to the gospel ministry because he believed that ordination by man did not determine one's calling. He believed that the only necessary ordination was that of God. He facetiously said that most ordinations were merely "placing empty hands on empty heads."[4] He saw no precedent for such a ceremony in Scripture and was disinclined to endorse a practice that sought to convey authority from one man to another. He detested the "dogma of apostolic succession" that the Anglicans practiced, and ordination was an important part of that policy. He held to that position throughout his ministry. Interestingly enough, evangelist D. L. Moody, an ardent admirer of Spurgeon, followed his example and refused ordination.

Spurgeon also refused the title *Reverend* because he believed that he was unworthy of such a title. He preferred to be called Mr. Spurgeon or Pastor

Spurgeon. He said, *"Reverend* and *sinner* make a curious combination; and I know I am the second, I repudiate the first."[5] The lack of the title, however, never seemed to hinder him; in fact, it furthered his reputation as the preacher to the common man. How different his attitude was in contrast to ambitious leaders today who seek professional recognition and resort to obtaining mail-order doctorates to obtain status.

Spurgeon refused to use musical instruments in the church, believing that they added nothing to the singing of the people alone. A pitch pipe was used to signal the beginning of each hymn. Spurgeon was so adamant about this point that he would not even allow the great song leader Ira Sankey, who accompanied D. L. Moody in his evangelistic campaigns, to sing with an instrument in the Tabernacle. Sankey would eventually do so, although Spurgeon was not involved in the decision, when the American played and sang at Spurgeon's funeral at the Metropolitan Tabernacle.

Spurgeon was definitely a Nonconformist in the purest sense of the word. He rejected many of the general conventions of his day. For that he received considerable criticism because some people thought that he resisted conformity just to make a statement. Others believed that he demonstrated incredible arrogance. Spurgeon's response was simple: he thought that conventions, if they stood in the way of kingdom progress, were a sin.[6]

Creative Communication

Spurgeon employed in his preaching every means possible to attract and keep his hearers' attention. Why was he different? Part of it was a reflection of his cultural background, his Puritan roots, and his being a country lad from Essex. But, more than that, Spurgeon had a vibrant, dynamic faith that informed his total life and being. He was different than the typical preacher in that he ascertained the importance of direct and dynamic communication. To that end, he would go to any length to communicate the gospel to his hearers. He was reported to have said, "I am not very scrupulous about the means I use for doing good. . . . I would preach standing on my head, if I thought I could convert your souls."[7]

Great crowds of people and noted critics quickly realized his gift of speaking. The prominent actor Sheridan Knowles said of him,

He is only a boy, but he is the most wonderful preacher in the world.

He is absolutely perfect in oratory, and beside that, a master in the
art of acting. He has nothing to learn from me or anyone else. He is
simply perfect. He knows everything. He can do anything. . . . Why,
boys, he can do anything he pleased with his audience! He can make
them laugh and cry and laugh again in five minutes. His power was
never equalled.[8]

Simple, Yet Eloquent

Great numbers of people responded to the gospel message that Spurgeon
proclaimed simply but eloquently. One biographer characterized his preaching thus:

Simplicity and clearness were characteristic of all of his discourses.
It was his aim to so preach that the least instructed of his congregation should grasp his meaning and remember what he said.[9]

The designation of Spurgeon as "the Prince of Preachers" is no accident.
Spurgeon, in both his natural abilities and his determination to draw people
to Christ, combined all of his creative resources to become perhaps the best
communicator of his time. From the time of his youth, Spurgeon received
many accolades as admirers noted his powerful voice, his excellent elocution,
his enrapturing style, his pictorial language, his dramatic gestures, and most
of all the profound truth of his preaching.

His Broad Appeal

The evidence of Spurgeon's broad appeal was in the many different types of
people who came to hear him. Because of Spurgeon's popularity, his congregation each week consisted of the committed, the curious, the skeptical, the
seeking—regardless of place in life or cultural upbringing. One early biographer contended that Spurgeon's "chief aim was to attract great crowds and
arrest their attention to the claims of religion. With this end he made his sermons as striking and startling as possible."[10]

He reached people of varied intellect and social class through his preaching—
the working classes, consisting of artisans and tradesmen, as well as the middle
class and academic types. In fact, once Spurgeon wrote to a friend telling him

about "a harlot of the deepest dye" that was converted. She wrote to him to tell of her salvation. Spurgeon responded, "Isn't that glorious! This is the sort of thing I like to live for."[11] This one example is indicative of Spurgeon's ability to reach people of varying stations in life. As one pamphleteer noted, Spurgeon was preeminently "the preacher of the people."[12]

What was the substance of Spurgeon's preaching? It was a solid exposition of biblical truth. He preached to people in their life situations. He had great confidence in the spiritual discernment of his "common" hearers. An article in a newspaper of the time stated, "Mr. Spurgeon speaks in a lively graphic and impressive style. His home Saxon is full of pith and vigour. He cannot, we should think, be misunderstood, and very rarely can there be in his audience a sleepy hearer."[13] He represented the historical transition from the ornate, Latinized oratorical style in vogue at the time to a simple, natural Anglo-Saxon communicative style.[14]

Manners and Methods

Spurgeon used illustrations that were alive, relevant, and practical. He used copious personal experiences, and he was often criticized for using them. He was accused of being egotistical. For example, one of his detractors said, his preaching and writing were "dominated by his own experience, his advice, his testimony, his character. When his own experience is not cited, then the reader must endure the testimony of his wife, his sons, his grandfather. . . . He missed no opportunity to promote his family or himself."[15] Spurgeon's model, however, was the apostle Paul, who often used himself as an example in writing to the churches. Thus, he justified his personal experiences and Christian pilgrimage to be a common element in his preaching.

Spurgeon emphasized to his students the need to be natural and interesting. He said of dull preachers, "They make good martyrs. They are so dry they burn well."[16] His avid reading and knowledge of current events contributed to the resourcefulness of his messages and their application to practical needs in his congregation. He used catchy sermon titles: "Turn or Burn," "The Monster Dragged to Light," "Sweet Comfort for Feeble Saints," "How Saints May Help the Devil," "Children Brought to Christ, Not the Font," "Christopathy," and *"Noli Me Tangere"* (Latin for "Touch Me Not"—a sermon on Mary, the mother of Jesus). Spurgeon was not afraid to "push the envelope" when it came to enlivening his preaching and whetting the appetites of his congregation.

Spurgeon was known for his dramatic gestures. In the early days, public critics labeled them "antics," "ginger-pop sermonizing," "pulpit buffoonery," "spiritual dram-drinking," and "blasphemous prayer" and used adjectives such as *arrogant, pretentious, crude, ignorant, theatrical,* and *impudent.* He was even called "the Barnum of the pulpit."[17] Spurgeon was amused by many of the characterizations and formed a scrapbook of clippings titled "Facts, Fiction and Facetiae," which he enjoyed showing to visitors who came calling.

One of the many cartoons published at that time was titled "Brimstone & Treacle." Treacle was the average minister of the day, depicted as a meek, bespectacled cleric reading his sermon from a full manuscript. Brimstone was Spurgeon, his arms flung apart and his face the image of vivacity, typifying daring and directness. Not everyone evaluated Spurgeon's creative style positively. Author George Eliot, for example, once visited the Tabernacle and characterized Spurgeon's preaching as "a most superficial grocer's back-parlour view of Calvinistic Christianity."[18]

Everything considered, however, Spurgeon's style of communication was creative and energizing to the throngs who heard him. He quickly gained their attention, and in a lively manner, communicated the message that God had given him for the occasion.

Evangelistic Methodologies

Spurgeon spoke at the Metropolitan Tabernacle on the one hundredth anniversary of William Carey's birth. He referred to Carey, who birthed the modern missionary movement, as "chief among the discoverers and innovators who were worthy of honour."[19] He challenged his hearers:

> When a man once had a good thought, he should not be afraid of it because nobody else had thought of it. He should do it and dare it, defying custom if it thwarted him, tearing it to pieces if it stood in the way of right. All God's true servants were innovators. Those that turned the world upside down were the very descendants of the Lord Jesus Christ.[20]

Spurgeon no doubt thought of Carey as he utilized new evangelism methodologies and pursued new ideas for ministry. Just like Carey pioneered mission work in India, Spurgeon pioneered a new era of evangelism.

Advertising

Spurgeon believed in using publicity, which was considered unorthodox for his time. Early in his London ministry, he began to use handbills and posters to advertise his sermons and meetings. The populace considered such advertising to be worldly, much like the advertising that was used by circuses and theaters. Spurgeon disregarded the charge that he was doing such for the purpose of sensationalism. His methods worked for his purposes, and the crowds came to hear him in massive throngs, thus enabling him to communicate the gospel to many people. Spurgeon hardly ever turned down a chance to preach, whether it was in the open-air, on the street, in a public facility, or wherever he could gain hearers.

Using Public Halls

Another innovation credited to Spurgeon was the hiring of secular halls for holding worship services. During the time when his church at New Park Street was being enlarged and renovated, it was necessary for the church to secure an alternative facility for worship and preaching. Exeter Hall, which seated five thousand people, became the church's home for a number of months. It was filled to capacity from the opening service. The Royal Surrey Gardens Music Hall was another secular venue that the church used for special worship services to accommodate the crowds because it held more than ten thousand people.

As Spurgeon's fame spread among London circles, thousands of people came to hear him preach. Spurgeon disregarded the criticism that he was using "the Devil's house" for services. One publication criticized him thus:

> This hiring of places of public amusement for Sunday preaching is a novelty, and a painful one. It looks as if religion were at its last shift. It is a confession of weakness rather than a sign of strength. It is not wrestling with Satan in his strongholds,—to use the old earnest Puritan language;—but entering into a very cowardly truce and alliance with the world.[21]

On the contrary, Spurgeon was thrilled to proclaim the gospel in a setting that was otherwise used for purposes of the world. The culmination of his secular preaching was the invitation to preach to a massive audience of 23,654 at a day of national prayer at Crystal Palace.

Inquirers Meetings

He made himself available on Tuesday afternoons for "inquirers" at the Tabernacle. "Whenever I was able to appoint a time for seeing converts and inquirers, it was seldom, if ever, that I waited in vain, and, so many came, that I was quite overwhelmed with gratitude and thanksgiving to God."[22] He shared the following incident about two sisters:

> Two inquiring ones came to me in my vestry. They had been hearing the gospel from me for only a short season, but they had been deeply impressed by it. They expressed their regret that they were about to remove far away, but they added their gratitude that they had heard me at all. I was cheered by their kind thanks, but felt anxious that a more effectual work should be wrought in them, and therefore I asked them, "*Have* you in very deed believed in the Lord Jesus Christ? Are you saved?" One of them replied, "*I* have been trying hard to believe." This statement I have often heard, but I will never let it go by me unchallenged. "*No*," I said, "*that* will not do. Did you ever tell your father that you tried to believe him?" After I had dwelt a while upon the matter, they admitted that such language would have been an insult to their father. I then set the gospel very plainly before them in as simple language as I could, and I begged them to believe Jesus, who is more worthy of faith than the best of fathers. One of them replied, "*I* cannot realize it; I cannot realize that I am saved." Then I went on to say, "God bears testimony to his Son, that whosoever trusts in his Son is saved. Will you make him a liar now, or will you believe his word?" While I thus spoke, one of them started as if astonished, and she startled us all as she cried, "O sir, I see it all; I am saved! Oh, do bless Jesus for me; he has shown me the way, and he has saved me! I see it all." The esteemed sister who had brought these young friends to me knelt down with them while, with all our hearts, we blessed and magnified the Lord for a soul brought into light.[23]

Most British churches, unlike their American counterparts, did not extend an invitation for individuals to respond publicly to the gospel message in any manner after each service. Spurgeon, however, led his church to conduct "inquirers meetings" occasionally. These were organized for the purpose of counseling those who were anxious about their spiritual condition. As well, he held instruction classes for new believers. The elders were then sent as "messengers" to interview new church members, and then the candidates were presented to the church at a regular business meeting.

Through dynamic preaching, innovative evangelism, and the power of the Holy Spirit, Spurgeon's church grew to mammoth proportions for its time. In reality, Spurgeon's Metropolitan Tabernacle became the first megachurch of the modern era. In its day, it was the largest evangelical church in the world, attaining 5,284 members by 1871, just eighteen years into Spurgeon's London ministry.

Administrative Nuances

Among other new practices for his time, Spurgeon also used fundraising events, such as bazaars, which enabled him to open the newly constructed Metropolitan Tabernacle completely free of debt. Such events also were used to build new chapels in and around London.

Very few churches in the Victorian era kept statistical records of their growth and attendance. Spurgeon, however, kept detailed membership and baptismal records to track the church's phenomenal growth. Spurgeon also began the innovative practice of planting churches, sending students out to areas around London and other parts of the country to establish new works.

Spurgeon started the publication of a monthly magazine called *The Sword and the Trowel* at the Metropolitan Tabernacle. He named it such in his effort to communicate "a record of combat with sin and labour for the Lord."[24] Spurgeon did not think that the hymnbooks of his day were complete, so he compiled "Our Own Hymn Book." It contained both the hymns of others and some that the pastor himself penned.

Baptists have two ordinances, believer's baptism by immersion and the observance of the Lord's Supper. Unlike many Baptist churches in his time, Spurgeon's church practiced open communion, allowing all believers who were present to participate. Someone once challenged him about his restriction for church membership, which required baptism by immersion. Spurgeon told him about their open communion policy.

The man replied, "So, they're good enough for God, but not good enough for you." On that rare occasion, Spurgeon had no real reply. But his openness in communion participation challenged other churches in their own practice of the ordinance.

Educational Endeavors

Spurgeon's entrepreneurial spirit led him to found The Pastors' College, with the primary goal of equipping ministers with practical skills for the ministry. In his own words,

> When it was commenced, I had not even a remote idea of whereunto it would grow. There were springing up around me, as my own spiritual children, many earnest young men who felt an irresistible impulse to preach the gospel; and yet, with half an eye, it could be seen that their want of education would be a sad hindrance to them. It was not in my heart to bid them cease their preaching; and, had I done so, they would, in all probability, have ignored, my recommendation. As it seemed that they would preach, though their attainments were very slender, no other course was open but to give them an opportunity to educate themselves for the work.[25]

In the introduction to *Lectures to My Students*, Spurgeon shared why he thought it necessary to teach students about preaching from the heart of his own experience:

> The age has become intensely practical, and needs a ministry not only orthodox and spiritual, but also natural in utterance, and practically shrewd. . . . The solemn work with which the Christian ministry concerns itself demands a man's all, and that all at its best. . . . Therefore have I sought out to speak my whole soul, in the hope that I might not create or foster dullness in others.[26]

Many of his lectures to his students revolved around the call to preach and developing one's ability to communicate the Word of God effectively. Spurgeon covered many topics, dealing with everything from the substance of sermons and the choice of a text to spiritualizing; developing the voice; keeping attention; preaching for a decision; posture, action, and gestures; and using illustrations, anecdotes, and other resources for preaching. He even dealt with the physical aspects of a preacher, titling one lecture "To Workers with Slender Apparatus." Although the lectures might be dated in some of their specific applications, the heart of the lectures addresses matters of importance to all preachers regardless of the times.

Spurgeon was concerned about the development of one's speaking skills as a preacher. He did not recommend "impromptu speech" as a general rule. He counseled ministers to give themselves to preparation and an "instructive ministry"; otherwise, there might be a "vacuum in the meeting-house."[27] On the other hand, he warned against overpreparation and sacrificing "living zeal" for the sake of "studied composition." He asked, "Do you not think that many sermons are 'prepared' until the juice is crushed out of them, and zeal could not remain in such dry husks?"[28]

Spurgeon advocated that each preacher "prepare to the utmost" but avoid "injurious toil" that would dry it to death! He believed the Lord was more concerned about dynamic truth than "classical composition." In his estimation, the Spirit was more apt to speak through a message that was lively and experiential than one noted for its proper rhetoric. He wrote, "If there is fire, life, and truth in the sermon, then the quickening Spirit will work by it, but not else. Be earnest, and you need not be elegant."[29]

Other Innovations

Spurgeon blended evangelism and social concern perfectly. In fact, most philanthropic movements in the nineteenth century originated with evangelicals. Spurgeon saw society as an organic whole. He built almshouses for the poor (only one was in existence when he came to London). He built seventeen houses for the aged and a school for four hundred children. He erected the Stockwell Orphanage for homeless children. He began the Colportage Ministry to provide books for poor rural pastors. He instituted the Pastor's Aid Society to help the poor. He also founded the Old Ladies Homes, the Book Fund Ministry, the Rock Loan Tract Society, the Ladies Maternal Society, the Metropolitan Tabernacle Poor Minister's Clothing Society, the Flower Mission, the Baptist Country Mission, Mrs. Thomas's Mothers Mission, Mrs. Evan's

Home and Foreign Missionary Working Society, the Gospel Temperance Society, the Tract Society, the ragged schools, the Pioneer Mission, and other ministries. They all fit his approach to bringing the whole gospel to affect the whole person in every area of life.

The Risks of Creativity

Being creative can be risky business for some unsuspecting leaders. Many pastors go off to conferences and leadership seminars, get inspired, return to their churches, and seek to implement their newly discovered ideas only to experience defeat and rejection. It reminds me of Keating, the English professor played by Robin Williams in the movie *Dead Poets Society*. He tells his students dramatically, "*Carpe diem*—'Seize the day!' Every one of you will die," he warns, "and the critical question is Will you wait too long to make what you should of your lives? Make your life extraordinary!" Keating's students responded enthusiastically to his creative challenge. The climax of the film is the suicide death of Neil, one of Keating's brightest students, who is driven to despair by a father who insists that he excel academically so he can go to Harvard, but in the process he must give up his hopes of pursuing a career in theater. In a powerful scene that is full of Christian symbolism, Neil dies. Of course, Keating is dismissed. His creative passion in teaching was his undoing.

Perhaps not everyone under your leadership will respond to your creative approaches. One must proceed cautiously in certain situations. Spurgeon was fortunate in that he attained a massive following in a relatively short period of time, and popular support enabled him to provide bold and creative leadership in his ministry. The Christian leader is encouraged to exercise his spiritual gifts and pursue his creativity, but be ever mindful that some bumps might occur in the road along the journey of creative leadership.

One further note of warning regarding creativity and innovation is that serious problems occur within the church when one departs from biblical patterns, principles, and practices by introducing or allowing methods of the world that compromise the revelation of God. Creativity and innovation can be a very positive force for good, but, in the effort to attract more people, the Christian leader must always be alert as to things that divert from the gospel of Christ.

Developing One's Creativity

What gets your creative juices flowing? Some leaders are naturally more creative than others, but any leader can learn to become more creative. What can you do to facilitate creativity? Consider the following possibilities:

1. Develop a childlike sense of wonder. Take a unique interest in things that seem normal. Observe a child, and let the child in you notice the way the child's sense of awe is aroused through nature, insects, objects, and people.
2. Pursue your curiosity. Research and discover; study and dissect new ways to approach old problems.
3. Stretch your imagination. Meditate afresh on familiar Bible passages, and let the Lord challenge you anew.
4. Be willing to take risks. Step out of your comfort zone and attempt something unique (as long as it doesn't compromise biblical principles).
5. Associate with creative people. Creativity is contagious! You will catch it from others who will inspire you through their own creative processes and energies.
6. Find a place outside the office where you can think creatively. Often, your mind will be stimulated to fresh ideas through a different environment.
7. Pray and believe that God will help you to be more creative in your ministry. A most creative God wants to energize the creative potential in your life.

SPURGEON LEADERSHIP LESSONS

- **A creative God calls creative leaders to exercise creativity in their work for His kingdom.** C. H. Spurgeon believed fully in infinite possibilities and used all of his creative energies to communicate the gospel.
- **The message of the gospel does not change, but the manner of its presentation may be adapted according to the situation.** Spurgeon said, "I am not very scrupulous about the means I use for doing good.□.□.□. I would preach standing on my head, if I thought I could convert your souls."
- **A leader is not obligated to observe conventions simply as a matter of compliance.** They should be retained only if the cause merits it. Spurgeon thought that conventions, if they stood in the way of kingdom progress, were a sin.
- **A leader's personal distinctions should be determined by their alignment with his goals for the organization.** Spurgeon pursued many innovative methods because he believed them to be essential to spreading the gospel.
- **A leader can be as creative as possible as long as it doesn't compromise the message of the gospel.** Spurgeon would go to any length to communicate the gospel to his hearers, whether it was throwing tracts from train windows or advertising his services through secular media.
- **A leader should check his motivation regarding the effect that he seeks to create through his particular style of ministry.** Spurgeon's aim was to bring glory to God, not to attract people to himself.
- **A leader's creativity should be a reflection of his own gifts and abilities.** Spurgeon's ministry with innovative applications was a fulfillment of the faithful and creative application of his spiritual gifts.
- **Being creative can be risky business for some unsuspecting leaders.** Spurgeon was savvy enough to employ innovations that were bolstered by his popular support.
- **Leaders who are discoverers and innovators are worthy of honor.** Spurgeon, speaking of missionary founder William Carey, stated: "All God's true servants were innovators. Those that turned the world upside down were the very descendants of the Lord Jesus Christ."

10

COMPASSION

Personal Toughness and Pastoral Tenderness

With all his maturity and firmness, the spiritual father is full of
tenderness, and manifests an intense love for the souls of men.
His doctrinal divinity does not dry up his humanity. He was
born on purpose to care for other people, and his heart cannot
rest until it is full of such care.[1]

A strong leader who is committed to providing the best possible Christian leadership will demonstrate a balance between personal toughness and pastoral tenderness. He is able to show sensitive compassion to his followers. Compassion might seem to be a weak leadership trait to those secular critics who believe that there is no substitute for tough leadership if one desires to be effective. Their view includes the traditional notion that macho authoritarian leaders personify the survival of the fittest, winner-take-all in a dog-eat-dog world. In that sense, Spurgeon does not fit the mold.

True, the pastor of the Metropolitan Tabernacle was authoritarian to a great extent. He became known as the "Guv'nor." He said, "There must be only one captain in a ship."[2] He wielded a certain amount of power and could exercise it if necessary. But he never lorded it over his staff, his congregation, or even his students at The Pastors' College. Spurgeon's leadership was tempered with love. He was able to balance the strength of his convictions with the complement of a loving spirit. Although he had a reputation for and a public image of strong convictions, he was also regarded as a man with a compassionate heart. He developed personal toughness in spiritual matters, aided by the criticism and conflict that he suffered early in his London ministry. But he also showed pastoral tenderness when he encountered the failings of erring saints throughout his ministry.

He set high moral standards for himself and for other leaders, but at the same time he understood the complexities of maintaining those standards. Although he was resolute in his personal discipline, Spurgeon was extremely sensitive when it came to exercising the role of disciplinarian in his pastoral relationships. That is where we see his true sense of compassion. He wrote, "If we would save our hearers from the wrath to come, we must realize that they are our brothers. We must have sympathy with them, and anxiety about them; in a word, passion and compassion. May God grant these to us!"[3]

Servant Leadership

The concept of servant leadership is well known among Christians. Jesus set the best example for us as the one who came not to be served, but to serve and give His life "as a ransom for many." When His disciples bickered about who was going to be greatest in His kingdom, Jesus reminded them that the greatest among them must be the servant of all. Can one be powerful and humble? A leader and a servant? Wasn't Jesus? Yes, he was *powerful*—He calmed the storm on the sea. He also was *humble*—He submitted to death on a cross. Yes, He was a *leader*—He said, "Take up your cross and follow me." But He was also a *servant*—He washed the disciples' feet.

Spurgeon believed that leaders must first be servants. When they became servants, it placed them in a position from which they could lead. He wrote,

> Let us remember that we are the servants in our Lord's house. "Who-soever will be chief among you, let him be your servant." Let us be willing to be door-mats at our Master's entrance-hall. Let us not seek honor for ourselves, but put honor upon the weaker vessels by our care for them. . . . In our Lord's Church, let the poor, the feeble, the distressed have the place of honor, and let us who are strong bear their infirmities. He is highest who makes himself lowest; he is greatest who makes himself less than the least.[4]

Responsibilities or Rights?

What, then, should the Christian leader who wants to exert influence among his followers do? First, he must realize that a price has to be paid. It is really about giving yourself. Leighton Ford writes, "Jesus knew the price of leadership—he was willing to give himself."[5] The concept of servant leadership is certainly apparent here. It implies that we are more conscious of our *responsibilities* than our *rights*. Far too many pastors and leaders are more concerned today about their personal rights and attainments than they are their responsibilities before God to their people. They are more interested in what they can gain than what they can give.

A servant leader, on the other hand, will go to any length to provide the leadership that brings glory to God and builds up his people rather than himself. Spurgeon said, "We are MINISTERS. The word has a very respectable sound. To be a minister, is the aspiration of many a youth. Perhaps, if the word were otherwise rendered, their ambition might cool. Ministers are servants: they are not guests, but waiters; not landlords, but labourers."[6]

One such person in the secular world was Robert K. Greenleaf, who adapted the concept of servant leadership when he was director of management research for AT&T. For Greenleaf, leadership is a state of being, where the most fundamental value is the choice to serve, and where the commitment to a higher purpose becomes the source of resourceful and productive relationships between leader and followers.[7] Greenleaf believed that the role of the organizational leader was fulfilled in serving others—employees, customers, and community to establish a sense of community and share decision making while, at the same time, setting high standards and leading by example.

Pastoral Care

The Christian leader who ministers effectively to his followers understands that pastoral care has to be a priority. It is really about nurturing relationships. If a pastor/leader is a shepherd, he must understand the condition of his flock. Proverbs 27:23 says, "Be sure you know the condition of your flocks, give careful attention to your herds" (NIV). It is your business to know how the sheep are doing. Jesus is the Chief Shepherd, and the local pastor serves as an undershepherd to his flock, the local church.

Spurgeon's primary role as a leader was as a shepherd to his flock at the Metropolitan Tabernacle. He kept this functioning pastoral role uppermost in his service to the Lord. He devoted himself to knowing his people and was concerned to meet the needs of his congregation. He wrote, "Take care to be on most familiar terms with those whose souls are committed to your care. Stand in the stream and fish. Many preachers are utterly ignorant as to how the bulk of people are living; they are at home among books, but quite at sea among men."[8]

Cultivating Nurturing Relationships

It's important that adequate time in preparation and prayer is maintained in the study. But the pastor must make a priority to be out among the people to whom God has called him to serve. Too often, pastors adopt a professional stance whereby they believe that their first priority is preparing sermons and Bible studies. They are prone to delegate to others much, if not most, of the hospital calling, visitation, and counseling, believing that they are best serving their congregation in the study. They must beware lest they fail to cultivate nurturing relationships with the people to whom they minister.

Our responsibility as leaders is to nurture the people of God. We nurture them by giving encouragement and spiritual counsel. We provide crisis ministry when it is needed in times of death, divorce, illness, and tragedy. We ensure that we are there for our followers during the important passages of life—birth, marriage, and death. We are present to share in the sorrows as well as the joys of life.

Spurgeon loved his people and ensured that they knew that he loved and cared for them. When instructing other ministers, he wrote, "Brethren, let us heartily love all whom Jesus loves. Cherish the tried and suffering. Visit the fatherless and the widow. Care for the faint and the feeble. Bear with the melancholy and despondent. Be mindful of all parts of the household, and thus shall you be a good shepherd."[9]

Being Transparent and Vulnerable

Ministering from weakness is a unique way that a leader shows concern for his followers. So often, however, leaders feel compelled to put forth an image that they cannot live up to. They want their followers to know that they are strong and healthy and have things under control.

Spurgeon, from the time he was twenty-four, suffered from rheumatic gout and often had to be away from his pulpit and people to recuperate. He once stated that he feared his congregation would no longer want a poor crippled pastor. One of his deacons replied, "Why, my dear sir, we would sooner have you for one month in the year than anyone else in the world for the whole twelve months."[10]

Spurgeon was transparent and vulnerable before his people and willing to be open about his personal struggles. His church identified with his frailties and weaknesses and was able to offer reciprocal empathy for their ailing pastor.

Spurgeon's great accomplishments as a pastor are a tribute to the way in which he related to his members. Through close to thirty-eight years of ministry, he earned their trust and devotion. He honored them by his leadership and entrusted many of them with ministry responsibilities that equipped them in their service to the Lord. He felt an obligation to be their spiritual father, encouraging them with the attention of a devoted father. He wrote, "With all his maturity and firmness, the spiritual father is full of tenderness. . . . He was born on purpose to care for other people, and his heart cannot rest until it is full of such care."[11]

The crucial importance of a leader's relationship to his followers has been known for a long time. Chinese philosopher Dao Teh Ching wrote five hundred years before Christ, "A leader is best when people barely know that he exists, not so good when people obey and acclaim him, worse when they despise him. Fail to honor people, they fail to honor you; but of a good leader, who talks little when his work is done, his aim fulfilled, they will all say, 'We did this ourselves.'"[12] When a pastor equips his people with the right ministry tools and then releases them for ministry, they will accomplish much in their service to Christ.

Redemptive Concern

A Christian leader must have redemptive concern for his followers. Spurgeon demonstrated such concern for his people throughout his extensive ministry. Of course, his greatest concern was for the salvation of their souls. He wrote, "If we be in Christ's stead, we shall not bully, but tenderly persuade. We shall have true sympathy, and so we shall plead with sinners unto tears, as though their ruin were our woe, and their salvation would be our bliss."[13]

Spurgeon had an undying passion to see people come to faith in Christ, and it grieved him to see them self-destruct in their sinful lifestyles. So, he used every available means to communicate the urgency of their need to respond when the conviction of the Holy Spirit came upon them.

Unconditional Love

A redemptive leader is characterized by "unconditional love." Unconditional love says, "You have done nothing and can do nothing that will prevent my loving you." This does not mean that you condone one's actions or wink at sin. If moral failure occurs, you must address it. If a relationship fails, you must confront it. If someone fails in a responsibility, you must correct that person. Spurgeon wrote, "Better far will it be for us to find fault with ourselves rather than with our people, when there is anything wrong with them. Still, our church members are men, and the best of men are but men at the best; to direct, instruct, console, and aid so many different minds, is no easy task."[14]

Spurgeon, in a lecture to his college students, shared an incident about his dilemma regarding an erring brother in the ministry:

> I am bowed to the very dust when I fear that any brother is erring in doctrine, lacking in grace, or loose in behavior. . . . Just now, one brother, by his general self-indulgent habits, has lost the respect of his people, and must move. I do not want to inflict a curse on another congregation, and I do not want to cast him off. Between these two courses, I am perplexed. Pray for me, for him, for all the brethren, and for yourselves.[15]

On one occasion, Spurgeon felt the need to upbraid one of his deacons. As he recounted it,

> One day I spoke rather sharply to one of them, and I think he deserved the rebuke I gave him; but he said to me: "Well, that may be so; but I tell you what, sir, I would die for you any day." "Oh," I replied, "bless your heart, I am sorry I was so sharp; but still, you did deserve it, did you not?" He smiled, and said he thought he did, and there the matter ended.[16]

The Capacity to Forgive

In all the matters of leadership, there must be the capacity for forgiveness. One must offer forgiveness, especially considering the forgiveness one has received from Christ. How do you know you've forgiven someone? Eugene

Habecker writes, (1) Don't keep bringing it up. (2) Don't tell others about the problem. (3) Don't dwell on it—let it go and move on.[17]

Forgiveness, accompanied by mercy, goes a long way in one's being a redemptive leader. Romans 12:8, referring to gifts, says, "if it is leadership, let him govern diligently; if it is showing mercy, let him do it cheerfully" (NIV). The context could lead us to interpret leadership as being linked to the gift of "showing mercy." Remember—*justice* is getting what we deserve, *grace* is getting what we don't deserve, and *mercy* is not getting what we do deserve. A leader who shows redemptive concern will administer mercy in his ministry.

At the same time, leaders who are arrogant and show little mercy to others must be careful lest they fall. The apostle Paul warned the Galatian leaders, "But watch yourself, or you also may be tempted" (Gal. 6:1 NIV). Leaders who show little care and understanding when another person falls might not see their own susceptibility and be carried off into the same sin. For those who think that they're above such temptations, they might be most vulnerable. In such cases, the danger consists in losing spiritual qualities that commend one for leadership.[18] Spurgeon wrote,

> A minister's wisdom lies in endeavouring to be wise for others, not cunning for himself. . . . I know a brother . . . the moment that he thinks that a member, especially a deacon, has gone wrong, he blows the whole thing to pieces, and calls it faithfulness. This is not acting . . . wise. . . . If we have wisdom, we shall maintain peace, and shall attempt reforms with gentleness.[19]

Respect for All Persons

Christian leaders maintain and promote diligently the dignity and worth of each individual. This means that we treat all people fairly, that we are willing to relate to "the least of these," and that we are equally accessible to all people.

Spurgeon cared about all of the people under his charge. He showed respect in his relationships, whether the person was a butcher or a member of parliament. He felt compelled to love them because he knew that Christ loved them. He wrote, "We must love sinners for Christ's sake. . . . The fallen, the frivolous, the captious, the indifferent, and even the malicious must share our love. We must love them to Jesus."[20]

Perhaps the best leader has the smallest ego. Truly, a leader is at his best when he is adding value to the lives of other people. Too many leaders have a problem with their ego. They are worried about their turf, concerned that someone else might get the credit, fearful that someone might try to usurp their position. Much can be accomplished if we don't care who gets the credit. Spurgeon wrote, "If we have great love to Jesus, and great compassion for perishing men, we shall not be puffed up with large success; but we shall sigh and cry over the thousands who are not converted."[21]

Respecting Leaders Who Serve with You

Spurgeon surrounded himself with competent people who were able to administer many of the functions of his ministries. He then let them do so, without constant interference from him. An effective leader must not only initiate well and finish well but also sustain well. Sensitive compassion is essential to sustaining leadership effectiveness. A leader pays diligent attention to the needs of his fellow leaders, as much as to the general followers. He spends quality time with them, equips them for their ministries, offers counsel and direction when it is needed, and gives them the respect they deserve.

The leader who demonstrates sensitive compassion will lead according to the servant model of Jesus, that is, the one who desires to be the greatest among men must be the servant of all. He will minister effectively to those in need through pastoral care. He will reach out to the lost through the urgency of redemptive concern. He will not discriminate against anyone but will respect every individual for whom Christ died. Although a leader must be as tough as nails when it comes to spiritual fortitude, let him be as soft as silk when it comes to sharing the compassion of Jesus Christ.

SPURGEON'S LEADERSHIP LESSONS

- **Effective leaders balance "strong convictions" with a loving spirit.**
  Although he was tough in personal discipline, Spurgeon was sensitive
  when it came to his pastoral role with people. He wrote, "With all his
  maturity and firmness, the spiritual father is full of tenderness, and manifests an intense love for the souls of men."
- **A leader who is committed to providing leadership that will include
  the best qualities of Christianity will demonstrate sensitive compassion in the process.** Spurgeon exhorted, "If we would save our hearers from the wrath to come, we must realize that they are our brothers.
  We must have sympathy with them, and anxiety about them; in a word,
  passion and compassion. May God grant these to us!"
- **The Christian leader who ministers effectively to his followers understands that pastoral care has to be a priority.** Spurgeon challenged ministers, "Take care to be on most familiar terms with those
  whose souls are committed to your care. Stand in the stream and fish.
  Many preachers are utterly ignorant as to how the bulk of people are
  living; they are at home among books, but quite at sea among men."
- **Spurgeon believed that leaders must first be servants. When they
  became servants, it placed them in a position from which they could
  lead.** "Let us remember that we are the servants in our Lord's house.
  'Whosoever will be chief among you, let him be your servant.' Let us be
  willing to be door-mats at our Master's entrance-hall. Let us not seek
  honor for ourselves, but put honor upon the weaker vessels by our care
  for them."
- **A Christian leader must have redemptive concern for his followers.**
  Spurgeon wrote, "If we be in Christ's stead, we shall not bully, but tenderly persuade. We shall have true sympathy, and so we shall plead with
  sinners unto tears, as though their ruin were our woe, and their salvation
  would be our bliss."
- **A redemptive leader is characterized by "unconditional love."**
  Spurgeon loved his people and ensured that they knew he loved and
  cared for them. When instructing other ministers, he wrote, "Brethren, let
  us heartily love all whom Jesus loves."
- **A leader shows real compassion by offering care and consolation
  to his followers.** Spurgeon counseled ministers, "Cherish the tried and
  suffering. Visit the fatherless and the widow. Care for the faint and the

feeble. Bear with the melancholy and despondent. Be mindful of all parts of the household, and thus shall you be a good shepherd."

- **Christian leaders maintain and promote diligently the dignity and worth of each individual.** "We must love sinners for Christ's sake. . . . The fallen, the frivolous, the captious, the indifferent, and even the malicious must share our love. We must love them to Jesus."

- **The greatest compassion that a Christian leader can show is a passion to lead someone to Christ.** To Spurgeon, that was the greatest goal: "If we have great love to Jesus, and great compassion for perishing men, we shall not be puffed up with large success; but we shall sigh and cry over the thousands who are not converted."

11

COMPASS

Leading Despite Criticism and Conflict

Controversy is never a very happy element for the child of God.
. . . But the soldier of Christ knows no choice in his Master's
commands. . . . The servant of Christ must endeavour to
maintain all the truth which his Master has revealed to him,
because as a Christian soldier, this is part of his duty.[1]

Any leader who is faithful to his calling sooner or later will find himself embroiled in conflict or controversy. Contrary to idealistic notions about leadership, even in the Christian context, leaders often discover resistance and reaction that they never anticipated when they accepted God's call. Before long, they find the following statements to be true.

1. A leader who pursues an aggressive agenda for change will have to handle inevitable organizational conflict among his followers.
2. A leader who is passionate about bringing people together for a common purpose will have to deal with personalities who seek to thwart his intentions.
3. A leader who stands for the cause of righteousness will no doubt create public reaction that might result in personal scrutiny and unjust criticism.

The leader who expects to make a difference must be prepared to encounter controversy en route to accomplishing the goals that he has set for the organization. Controversy might not become a familiar friend, but it will become an acquaintance that seems to turn up at the most inopportune times.

Spurgeon the Object of Controversy

C. H. Spurgeon was no stranger to controversy. Throughout much of his life, he attracted a significant amount of criticism and engaged in numerous controversies that revolved around his beliefs and the practice of the Christian faith. Indeed, at the beginning of his London ministry, when he was just nineteen years of age, one pamphleteer wrote, "At the present day . . . no living preacher gives rise to so much conversation and it may be added, so much controversy, as the Rev. C. H. Spurgeon."[2] From the beginning to the end of his ministry, Spurgeon recognized that controversy was an unavoidable consequence for a soldier of Christ battling for the causes of righteousness.

Today's ministers are sometimes guilty of seeking to do everything they can to avoid controversy, taking the course of least resistance if at all possible. But authentic Christian leaders will not shun all conflict and controversy if they seek to be faithful to their calling. Jesus counseled His disciples that because the world hated Him, the world would hate them as well. Why should godly leaders today expect that they deserve any better treatment than that given to the holy, perfect Son of God? Jesus was executed like a common criminal, even though He had committed no wrong whatsoever. We may very well suffer various types of persecution in the course of our ministry. But this should be expected, rather than come as a surprise, when we seek to lead effectively for the kingdom of Christ.

Controversy Within the Church

When I was in college, my father served as pastor of a small church in a rural town. In the course of his ministry, he discovered that one of his deacons was engaged in an illicit relationship. He confronted the deacon, who immediately turned on him, showing no sign of remorse or repentance. He and several of his friends launched a campaign of false rumors and innuendo against my father, which ultimately resulted in his dismissal by a one-vote majority at a church meeting. Although my father confronted the unrighteousness in his church that was well-known in the surrounding community, it resulted in his untimely dismissal. He was faithful to his calling, but it cost him dearly.

One too frequent result of church conflict today is forced termination of pastors/staff in ministry. The dismissal of pastors is much more prevalent among churches today than it was just a few decades ago. One reason is that the level of expectation in Christian leadership has risen over the years. Whereas in the past ministers were usually terminated because of heretical beliefs, moral failure, or financial improprieties, today one might be released for less offensive issues. Some pastors have been fired because the church wasn't growing fast enough or because of personality differences. Others have been let go because they forced issues of race, ministered to "different" types of people, neglected some of their regular pastoral duties, were perceived as unfriendly, or created changes in worship/music that the congregation found unacceptable.

Although controversy can arise through a leader's faithful service to Christ, some conflicts are brought on because of one's own faults and failures. Sometimes leaders can be tactless, careless, thoughtless, uncommunicative, headstrong, dictatorial, and arrogant—and they stir up conflict as a result. Jesus, in the Sermon on the Mount, stated that we are to be blessed if we suffer for righteousness' sake. But no blessing is promised to the unwise leader who is his own worst enemy. Carnal, self-generated controversy is neither admirable nor desirable. It only creates a roadblock on the journey to worthy accomplishments, a hazard that could be avoided through wiser leadership choices under the guidance of the Holy Spirit.

For the minister of the gospel, the challenge of controversy is to maintain one's integrity and assume appropriate responsibility for leadership with a goal to not only surviving but also thriving in an era of unprecedented expectations.

Public Controversy

Spurgeon was embroiled in a number of controversies in his lifetime. His first engagement in public controversy began when he became the subject of the Media Controversy during his early London ministry (1853–1856). This was followed by various other controversies: the "Rivulet" controversy (1856),[3] the "Divine Life in Man" controversy (1860),[4] the "Slavery Question" controversy (1860),[5] and the controversy with the Baptist Missionary Society (1863–1866).[6] Although each incident stirred up conflict and caused consternation among different Christian groups, no major rifts occurred between Spurgeon and other Christian leaders in England as a result of them.

Positive Benefits of Controversy

In some cases, leaders who receive public criticism for their controversial stands receive the positive benefit of the unity that it creates when their followers "close rank" behind their leader. In recent years, one might compare the relationship of Jerry Falwell (an often outspoken pastor who has drawn fire from the public sector on many occasions) and his church, Thomas Road Baptist Church in Lynchburg, Virginia, with that of Spurgeon and his church in London. Throughout Falwell's ministry, his church has stood solidly behind him and united with him in the causes that he espoused. In battles that have ranged from his opposition to abortion on demand to the promotion of alternative sexual lifestyles, Falwell and his church have presented a united front.

Similarly, Spurgeon's church rallied behind him when he was attacked in the press. Writing about the Media Controversy in his early ministry, he stated, "The bond that united me to the members of New Park Street was probably all the stronger because of the opposition and calumny that, for a time at least, they had to share with me."[7]

The Two Big Controversies

The two most prominent of Spurgeon's public controversies were the Baptismal Regeneration Controversy in 1864 and the Downgrade Controversy, which occurred in 1888, near the end of his ministry. Some attention was given in an earlier chapter to the Baptismal Regeneration Controversy, in which Spurgeon confronted the Church of England over its subscription to a prayer book that he believed allegedly conveyed salvation to infants upon their baptism. That conflict resulted in Spurgeon's withdrawal from the Evangelical Alliance and created strains between him and the Anglicans for some time to follow. It did not, however, hinder his affiliations with his own denomination; rather, it seemed to strengthen those ties and spur his own congregation to greater achievements. Such was not the case, however, in the final controversy of his life, the Downgrade Controversy. It is appropriate here to give some brief details concerning the public controversy that severed Spurgeon's ties to the Baptist Union.

The Downgrade Controversy

Spurgeon ministered among the ranks of fellow Baptists in union for more than forty years. As a teenager, because of his own scriptural convictions, Spurgeon broke rank with his family, who were Congregationalists, and joined a local Baptist fellowship. He was immersed happily, became involved in Baptist life, and continued as a loyal participant for many years to come. Yet, in the latter years of his ministry and in a relatively short period of time, the great preacher moved from a position of optimism and expectation to disillusionment and withdrawal from the fellowship of the Baptist Union. A rift was opened between pastor and denomination, never to be mended by the time of his death in 1892.

Articles in The Sword and the Trowel

The Downgrade Controversy took its name from a series of articles that suggested that orthodox Christianity was on the "down grade." In 1887, three anonymous articles were published in Spurgeon's church paper, *The Sword and the Trowel,* that dealt with various aspects of the decline of evangelical Christianity. The main goal of the articles was to show the dangers of apostasy from evangelical truth, a course described by one Baptist historian as that "which would lead to rationalism and disaster."[8] Spurgeon followed the articles with one of his own, describing the decline of evangelical doctrine among dissenters in general. He declared,

> The atonement is scouted, the inspiration of Scripture is derided, the Holy Spirit is degraded into an influence, the punishment of sin is turned into fiction, and the resurrection into a myth, and yet these enemies of our faith expect us to call them brethren and maintain a confederacy with them.[9]

Spurgeon's use of forthright, pungent phrases was bound to attract the notice of his readers. He responded by calling for some type of confessional statement among the Baptists, such as the declaration of faith adopted by the Evangelical Alliance. He hoped that such a statement might help to stem the tide of doctrinal compromise that he believed was becoming more prominent.

Spurgeon's Withdrawal from the Baptist Union

Although some official attention of the Baptist denomination was given to his initial concerns, the annual meeting in Sheffield in 1887 made no mention of the issue in its regular sessions. Spurgeon was dismayed to find that many of the younger ministers regarded his calls for reform as an old man's senile joke. Finally, in October of 1887, after pursuing a course that achieved little result, Spurgeon believed that the time was at hand for him to depart from the fellowship of the Baptist Union:

> With deep regret we abstain from assembling with those whom we dearly love and heartily respect, since it would involve us in a confederacy with those with whom we can have no communion with the Lord.[10]

Spurgeon's personal withdrawal from the Baptist Union was the official launching of the Downgrade Controversy. The Metropolitan Tabernacle voted to follow suit shortly thereafter. His resignation caused a sensation not only among Baptists but also among what seemed to be the whole religious world at the time. The press gave prominent attention to the matter, with headlines declaring the breakup of Nonconformist Christianity. In addition to the reaction of the press, public meetings were held in various places to discuss the breach of fellowship between Spurgeon and the Baptist Union. But the controversy raged on.

Effects of the Controversy

A flurry of activity occurred within the denomination to find a way in which Spurgeon could be lured back into the fold. A special meeting was arranged between Spurgeon and the officers of the Baptist Union, but no reconciliation occurred. Spurgeon refused to withdraw his resignation, and the Union officials declined his request to recommend an adoption of a doctrinal declaration similar to those of other evangelical groups of the day. The culmination of activities was the annual assembly, at which a motion was made concerning a declaration of faith. A vote was taken on an amended declaration, which had been footnoted, to appease the more liberal personnel of the Baptist Union. The motion passed overwhelmingly, but Spurgeon interpreted it as a personal censure. From that time, he no longer participated in official Baptist Union activities.

The Downgrade Controversy had some serious ramifications for the evangelistic ministry of C. H. Spurgeon. Whereas most of his ministry at the Metropolitan Tabernacle had born much evangelistic fruit, the controversy that clouded the final five years of his life was definitely a detracting factor. Spurgeon was increasingly unwell; clearly, his vital energies were sapped by his concerns over the controversy. It undoubtedly played a role in the declining statistics for baptisms and new memberships in the Metropolitan Tabernacle the last several years of Spurgeon's life.

Personal Criticism

Leaders who are on the receiving end of personal criticism often find it difficult to handle. Whether it is an attack on their leadership style or personality issues, it still hurts. Regardless of how mature in one's faith one is, criticism stings. It takes a determined person to stave off the insecurities and doubt that come when one is assailed personally or when one's motives are challenged and one's credibility is questioned. Stuart Biscoe wrote, "There is a fine line between being thin-skinned and hard-nosed.... To be a successful pastor one must have the mind of a scholar, the heart of a child, and the hide of a rhinoceros.... We must either get tough or we will be destroyed."[11] Spurgeon demonstrated all of these qualities to varying degrees.

Spurgeon's Use of Humor

From the time he was a boy preacher at Waterbeach, Spurgeon had learned how to manage conflict. One of his methods was to use humor to disarm his critics. Early on, he was warned about a certain quarrelsome woman and told that she intended to give him a tongue-lashing. "All right," he replied, "but that's a game that two can play." Not long afterward, she met him and assailed him with a flood of abuse. He smiled and said, "Yes, thank you, I am quite well. I hope you are the same."[12] Spurgeon continued:

> Then came another outburst of vituperation, pitched in a still higher key, to which I replied, still smiling, "Yes, it does look rather as if it is going to rain; I think I had better be getting on." "Bless the man!"

she exclaimed, "he's as deaf as a post; what's the use of storming at him?" So I bade her, "Good morning," and I am not sure whether she ever came to the chapel to hear the "deaf" preacher who knew it was no use to give any heed to her mad ravings.[13]

Humor did not always fit the bill, though, when it came to dealing with personal attacks. Spurgeon was besieged by the vilification of those who opposed him and his popularity violently when he first arrived in London. He suffered at the hands of those in both the secular and the religious press who criticized his theology.

Spurgeon was a Calvinist, but he differed from the hyper-Calvinists, who believed that the gospel should not be offered to a general audience of saved and unsaved. James Wells, pastor of the prominent Surrey Tabernacle in London, epitomized the criticism that came against Spurgeon for his open evangelistic methods. Wells, under the pseudonym of "Job," often attacked Spurgeon through the pages of a religious publication called *The Earthen Vessel.* He believed Spurgeon's ministry to be deceptive, and his most virulent invective questioned whether Spurgeon was even saved. The young pastor did not engage Wells publicly, but he did write privately to his fiancée Susannah, "I find much stir has been made by 'Job's' letter, and hosts of unknown persons have risen up on my behalf. It seems very likely that King James will shake his little throne by lifting his hand against one of the Lord's little ones."[14]

The Press Softening Toward Spurgeon

Spurgeon lamented the treatment that he was receiving in the press. But as time went on, things began to change. The vociferous attacks subsided. Spurgeon found himself in a unique position of adapting to the commendations that were beginning to come his way. He wrote,

A year ago, I was abused by everybody—to mention my name was to mention the most abominable buffoon that lived . . . but then God gave me souls by hundreds, who were added to my church, and in one year it was my happiness to see not less than a thousand personally who had been converted. I do not expect that now. My name is somewhat esteemed now, and the great ones of the earth think it no dishonour to sit at my feet; but this makes me fear lest my God should forsake me now that the world esteems me. I would rather be despised and slandered than ought else.[15]

Spurgeon's fears of God's abandonment were unfounded because in the years to follow his ministry continued to grow and his influence became greater in the capital city and beyond.

Spurgeon's Response to Personal Attacks

The pastor of the Metropolitan Tabernacle seldom defended himself when he was on the receiving end of personal criticism, whether it was in the secular press or from the pulpit of one of his contemporaries. But he did not hesitate in taking to task anyone who criticized the pastor of the Metropolitan Tabernacle. Spurgeon saw a distinction between the two—personal reputation and public office—because his position reflected the reputation of God's servant, whose office represented a higher calling.

When Joseph Parker wrote his open letter (which was published in a London paper) to Spurgeon after their falling-out in 1890, many people expected that Spurgeon would respond openly in return. The next night, at the midweek meeting at the Tabernacle, it was packed to overflowing with curious worshipers. Spurgeon strode up to the pulpit, and, instead of remarking about Parker's letter, only stated, "Thank God there are still a faithful *few* who stand by the teaching of the Old Book." Although the letter stirred many people in Spurgeon's church and drew forth much public comment, Spurgeon never replied to Parker. The matter ended there.

Organizational Conflict

The Christian leader today will undoubtedly find himself engaged in managing conflict within his organization. The local pastor might be involved in trying to resolve conflict between members, conflict over worship differences, conflict over the direction of ministry, conflict over leadership personalities, etc.

Spurgeon undoubtedly faced conflict in administrating his institutions, encountered differences among his organizations, and dealt with distractions within his church. Unfortunately, most of the historical treatment of those issues is either absent or minimized. Spurgeon's particular style of leadership no doubt kept much of the typical organizational conflict managed and under control.

Spurgeon's Success in Overcoming Organizational Woes

Several reasons may account for the lack of reported conflicts within Spurgeon's church and other organizations. First, Spurgeon was a strong, successful leader whose influence and legendary status continued to increase during the time of his thirty-eight-year ministry at the same church. He had earned the right to become the undisputed leader of the flock, and received deferential treatment in most matters over the course of time. His people affectionately referred to him as "the Guv'nor," a name that connoted more than just a term of endearment. He was the singular figurehead and the absolute authority for the Tabernacle and all of its extended ministries.

Beyond his own church, he had become an icon in the religious world. By the age of twenty-five, he had become such a celebrity that ceramic figures of him were sold in the shops of London. By the age of thirty, his sermons had been printed in most of the major languages of the world. These are just two of the ways in which Spurgeon's popularity reached "superstar" proportions. Spurgeon's unrivaled influence could have been dangerous for a man of lesser ethics and convictions. But he maintained a good balance in his leadership and did not lord his influence over his members in an unhealthy manner.

Second, Spurgeon surrounded himself with capable people who administered the college, the orphanage, the almshouses, and the church in a manner that demonstrated undying loyalty to their leader.

How Spurgeon Dealt with Troublemakers

Spurgeon had a knack for putting potential troublemakers to work in a profitable manner that benefited both themselves and the church. On his twenty-fifth anniversary at the Metropolitan Tabernacle, Spurgeon declared to his congregation,

> We love each other for Christ's sake, and for the truth's sake. . . . I do thank God for this, because I know there is more than enough of evil among us to cause, dissensions in our midst. . . . We are as imperfect a band of men as might be found, but we are one in Christ.

> We have each had to put up with the other, and to, bear and for-
> bear; and it does appear to me a wonder that so many imperfect
> people should get on so well together for so long. By faith, I read
> over the door of our Tabernacle this text, "When He giveth quiet-
> ness, who then can make trouble?" . . . I have been warned, some-
> times, by fellow-ministers who have had a member who has proved
> troublesome to them, and who wished to come into our midst. I
> have been told that I must watch him very carefully, for he would
> be sure to be a cause of anxiety to me; but I have answered, "No one
> ever troubles me; I do not let him." Many of these people, who are
> supposed to be so dangerous, only want something to do; they have
> too much energy to be unemployed. I set them to work, and they
> are no longer troublesome; if that does not cure them, I give them
> still more work to do.[16]

Spurgeon's philosophy was to take disruptive types and put them to work. The
more they were engaged in ministry, the less time they had to stir up strife in
the congregation.

> They have too much vigor for small places, and need to be where
> their powers can have full scope, for then they have less time to
> notice things with which they do not wholly agree. Possibly, my
> brethren, many of you do not sufficiently prize the peace which
> reigns in our church. Ah! You would value it if you lost it. Oh, how
> highly you would esteem it if strife and schism should ever come
> into our midst! You would look back upon the happy days we have
> had together with intense regret, and pray, "Lord, knit us together
> in unity again; send us love to each other once more;" for, in a
> church, love is the essential element of happiness.[17]

Spurgeon as a Controversialist

Spurgeon was not considered the greatest controversialist by some of his
biographers. Fullerton stated,

> Mr. Spurgeon was too earnest, too intent on the eternal meaning of
> things, too sure of his own standing, to be a good controversialist.

His instinct led him to conclusions that others approached only by logic, and he was therefore not apt to be too patient with those who debated every step of the way, or lost themselves in details, failing, as he judged, to see the wood because of the trees, and the city because of the houses.[18]

The biographers based their judgments on Spurgeon's capabilities in controversy more on style than on substance. This analysis occurred because they viewed the true Spurgeon as one whose ministry was not characterized by controversy. Indeed, Spurgeon certainly did not see controversy as a major focus of his ministry. As Fullerton stated, "he was a witness, not a debater."[19] His primary goal was always evangelism. In 1861, Spurgeon stated, with respect to his ministry,

Controversy is never a very happy element for the child of God: he would far rather be in communion with his Lord than be engaged in defending the faith, or in attacking error. But the soldier of Christ knows no choice in his Master's commands. . . . The servant of God must endeavour to maintain all the truth which his Master has revealed to him, because as a Christian soldier, this is part of his duty.[20]

For the better part of his ministry, Spurgeon preferred not to argue and quibble over theological disputations. Rather, his approach was to present simply and directly the gospel message and let it stand on its own merit. He told his readers,

I'd rather walk ten miles to get out of a dispute than half-a-mile to get into one. I have often been told to be bold, and I take the bull by the horns, but, as I rather think that the amusement is more pleasant than profitable, I shall leave it to those who are so cracked already that an ugly poke with a horn would not do damage to their skulls.[21]

In spite of his claims to avoid disputes, however, Spurgeon seemed unable to stay out of controversy. Because of his dogmatic views and his confidence in his theology and practice of Christianity, Spurgeon was prone to attract controversy. In some ways, this was true from the day he arrived in London until the day he died in Mentone.

In some ways, one might concede that Spurgeon was not a good controversialist in terms of public debate, presentation, and strategy. As Carlile stated, "He knew nothing of the arts and crafts of trimming and compromising. He said the thing that was in his heart and said it with crystal clearness."[22]

But Spurgeon's concern was not to be good at controversy. It was to stand for truth. Historically, his willingness to take that stand on issues that he deemed were crucial to the evangelical faith inspired and encouraged future generations to stand up and be counted for causes they believed to be true. His struggle became symbolic of the struggle for the gospel that every generation must face. It is a resolve to remain true to firm convictions, regardless of the immediate outcome, believing that, in the end, righteousness will prevail.

SPURGEON'S LEADERSHIP LESSONS

- **Controversy is unavoidable for the person who seeks to be faithful to the Lord's calling.** Spurgeon wrote, "Controversy is never a very happy element for the child of God. . . . But the soldier of Christ knows no choice in his Master's commands. . . ." Jesus counseled His disciples that because the world hated Him, the world would hate them as well. Even the most effective leader will encounter controversy along the way.
- **A leader should not seek out controversy for its own sake.** Spurgeon expressed his distaste for controversy: "I'd rather walk ten miles to get out of a dispute than half-a-mile to get into one."
- **Some conflicts occur because of a leader's own faults and failures.** When a leader is tactless, careless, thoughtless, uncommunicative, head-strong, dictatorial, and arrogant, he will attract criticism as a result. This kind of controversy is not admirable; rather, it represents unwise leadership approaches that create adverse reactions.
- **Controversy can serve to unite a leader with his followers.** This point was true in Spurgeon's early ministry when he was maligned by the media. "The bond that united me to the members of New Park Street was probably all the stronger because of the opposition and calumny that, for a time at least, they had to share with me."
- **The wise leader is capable of differentiating between personal and professional criticism.** Spurgeon did not typically respond to personal attacks, but he did respond when someone criticized the pastor of the Metropolitan Tabernacle. He showed more concern for his official role than for his personal reputation.
- **Leaders profit by giving their potential critics significant responsibility.** Spurgeon's philosophy was to take disruptive types and, in his words, "I set them to work and they are no longer troublesome; if that does not cure them, I give them still more work to do."
- **A leader's goal should not include becoming a master of controversy, but to become consistent in handling the truth.** Spurgeon may not have been the best controversialist, but his resolve was to remain true to firm convictions, regardless of the outcome, believing that righteousness will prevail in the end.

12

COPING

Dealing with Illness and Depression

*Neither goodness, nor greatness can
deliver you from affliction.*[1]

*There are dungeons underneath the Castle of Despair
as dreary as the abodes of the lost, and some of us
have been in them.*[2]

Leadership always comes with a cost. Often a toll is taken in the form of trials and tribulations that arise from the pressures of leadership and making tough decisions. But also to be reckoned with is the higher price that is paid in the personal well-being of the leader, from within. Stress and suffering can have a tremendous impact on the effectiveness of a leader.

In his striking book titled *The Sword of Suffering*, Dr. Stephen Olford recounted his own experience with diagnosis and treatment of non-Hodgkins lymphoma. Olford revealed his deepest thoughts and feelings regarding his own personal suffering. In his introduction, he related the prophecy regarding the infant Jesus, when an elderly man named Simon approached Mary at the temple on the occasion of Jesus' dedication: "Behold, this Child is destined for the fall and rising of many in Israel, and for a sign which will be spoken against (yes, a sword will pierce through your own soul also), that the thoughts of many hearts may be revealed" (Luke 2:34–35 NKJV).

That "sword of suffering" was much more than insults and rejection that Mary would observe during Jesus' lifetime; it would take the form of "the ultimate pain, horror, and soul-piercing experience of watching the child of her womb brutally nailed to a Roman cross."[3] Olford's example of the suffering of

Christ was instructive for dealing with his own situation, and it is enlightening for all leaders who seek to serve the Lord.

C. H. Spurgeon was no stranger to suffering. Throughout his life and ministry, he suffered greatly as he ministered for Christ. The stresses and strains of ministry, the great expectations upon him week after week, the deadlines for writing, and the weight of spiritual responsibility—all contributed to the suffering he experienced. This suffering was manifested in different ways during his lifetime. Although we have already discussed the outward trials that Spurgeon experienced through conflict and controversy, we must turn our attention to the sufferings that he experienced from within. Without undue simplification, one can characterize Spurgeon's personal suffering as physical, emotional, and, yes, spiritual—understanding that these trials were interspersed somewhat in their effects upon him.

The Reality of Suffering

Spurgeon believed that suffering was a normal part of the Christian life. He agreed with the apostle Paul that the Christian should expect to participate in "the fellowship of [Christ's] sufferings" (Phil. 3:10 KJV). To Spurgeon, suffering was not an unusual occurrence for the Christian but rather an integral part of one's spiritual journey. He did not expect or believe that he should be able to avoid tribulations on this earth.

> There is no escaping troubles. We are born into it as the sparks fly upward. When we are born the second time, though we inherit innumerable mercies, we are certainly born to another set of troubles. We enter upon spiritual trials, spiritual conflicts, spiritual pains, and so forth; thus we beget a double set of distresses, as well as twofold mercies. Even king David, "The man after God's own heart," was one who felt God's own hand of chastisement. . . . Neither goodness, nor greatness can deliver you from affliction.[4]

It's true that we live in a world that is full of "troubles" where there is suffering, sickness, and disease. The reality of the fall of man and the entrance of sin into the world brought with it a manifestation of suffering that we share with all of humanity. And yet, much of that suffering has to do with the natural consequences of our own sin. At other times, the suffering comes because we share in the consequences of the corporate sin of others. Indeed, the Scriptures tell us that all of creation groans for its redemption, making us aware that we are experiencing that which is common to the general plight of humanity while on this earth.

People might ask why a good God allows evil and suffering to occur in the world. Although we might not understand divine providence in all of these matters while on earth, we are confident that we will comprehend all of God's ways when we meet Him face to face in eternity. Meanwhile, we trust that the Lord wills good for His creation. Some of the suffering that we experience might be the result of the wrong choices that men before us made. Who knows what exists in our physical environment that contributes toward disease as a result of the wrongful dominion of man over many centuries? Chemicals, pollution, and contaminated water—all factors related to disease—have infected our environment for years. Also, according to God's Word, the sins of the parents are visited upon their children from generation to generation. We are dealing with the multiplication of sin and its consequences over thousands of years.

On the other hand, God may intentionally allow some suffering for the refinement of our spiritual lives. Spurgeon believed that God has a purpose for us in the midst of our sufferings. He also believed that if we experienced a "double set of distresses," the Lord would equal that with His "twofold mercies."

Physical Weakness

"When I am weak, then I am strong" (2 Cor. 12:10 NIV). The words of the apostle Paul bring encouragement to the Christian leader who struggles with weaknesses. C. H. Spurgeon was an author, educator, evangelist, pastor, and, for many years, a sufferer because of severe physical afflictions. The Spurgeon who is often portrayed as strong and robust, also had to deal with personal frailties in his life. For much of his lifetime, Spurgeon suffered from rheumatic gout and related problems. His physical constitution, although seemingly rugged and healthy in his early years, began to deteriorate even when he was a young adult.

The first real incident of illness recorded was an extended problem in the winter of 1858, when Spurgeon was only twenty-four years old. He was out of the pulpit for three weeks, and it seemed a foreshadowing of things to come.

Dearly-beloved Friends, I am a prisoner still. Weakness has suc-
ceeded pain, and languor of mind is the distressing result of this
prostration of my physical powers. It is the Lord's doing. In some
sense, I might say with Paul, "I am a prisoner of Jesus Christ." But,
ah! my bonds are more easy and less honorable to wear than his.
Instead of a dungeon, my lot is cast in an abode of comfort. I am
not restrained from my accustomed ministry by a chain forged by
man, but by the silken cord of God's providence; no rough jailer,
but loving relatives and friends attend upon me in these tedious
hours of my bondage. I beseech you therefore, my beloved, let your
many prayers to God on my behalf be each and all mingled with
thanksgiving. Gratitude should ever be used in devotion, like salt
of old was in sacrifice, "without prescribing how much."[5]

This occasion was the first of many times that illness affected Spurgeon's
ability to conduct his ministry. As the years went by, the frequency and extent
of his attacks increased. In the latter part of his life, he was unable to preach
from his pulpit for lengthy periods of time. His rheumatic gout affected him
so much that, even when he was able to preach, he did so with tremendous
pain. At times, he had to preach with his foot resting on a stool. On other
occasions, his pain became so intense that he had to leave the service before it
was completed. But, through his weakness, he was able to identify with and
minister to the hurting ones present in his congregation. He knew exactly what
suffering was, and was able to bolster their spirits through the strength and
comfort that the Lord offered to them through him. Although Spurgeon believed in and prayed for healing, he continued to suffer from physical affliction the rest of his life. Eventually, his rheumatic gout developed into Bright's
disease, a kidney ailment, which hastened his death at the age of fifty-seven.

Mrs. Spurgeon's Illness

Spurgeon had not only his own physical problems but also those of his
beloved wife, Susannah, who also suffered physical weakness for much of her
adult life. Because of complications that came from childbearing, she became
a virtual invalid at the age of thirty-three, a condition that had many ramifications for both her public and private life. Her public appearances were limited,
and she often was confined to her bed. Spurgeon entertained visitors at home

by himself on a number of occasions. One American visitor reported that while they strolled on the lawn, Mrs. Spurgeon waved to them from her upstairs room. Still, even with her limitations, she provided great emotional support to and involved herself in her husband's ministry in numerous ways, as we learned in an earlier chapter.

Emotional Stress

Often, great leaders who have risen to the apex of success have also succumbed to the nadir of failure, in their spirit if not in reality. Some of them have been plagued by personal issues that affected them their entire lives. Winston Churchill said, "Depression followed me around like a black dog all of my life."[6] Abraham Lincoln, when he was a young lawyer in Illinois, became so depressed that his friends reportedly had to hide knives and razors from him. He wrote concerning this problem, "I am now the most miserable man living. . . . Whether I shall be better, I cannot tell. I awfully forebode I shall not."[7] Churchill and Lincoln both became great leaders who were able to rise above their emotional weaknesses to lead effectively in times of great national duress.

Spurgeon was also known to suffer from depression. He once stated, "There are dungeons underneath the Castle of Despair as dreary as the abodes of the lost, and some of us have been in them."[8] That statement illustrates just how low he could get at times. His depression seemed to be an unavoidable occurrence in the emotional struggles of his life.

The Aftereffects of the Music Hall Incident

Mentioned earlier was the tragic occurrence at the opening service at the Music Hall at the Royal Surrey Gardens on October 19, 1856. The huge gathering of more than ten thousand people had just settled in for the service when "a disturbance was caused, and the congregation was seized with a sudden panic."[9] Seven people were trampled to death and several dozen others were injured after a spurious alarm of fire caused people to rush for the doors. The Metropolitan Tabernacle church-book contained the following entry regarding the tragedy:

> This lamentable circumstance produced very serious effects on the nervous system of our Pastor. He was entirely prostrated for some days,

and compelled to relinquish his preaching engagements. Through the great mercy of our Heavenly Father, he was, however, restored so as to be able to occupy the pulpit in our own chapel on Sunday, November 2nd, and gradually recovered his wonted health and vigour.[10]

After the Surrey Garden Music Hall incident, Spurgeon suffered panic attacks for the rest of his life. Any time he entered an overly crowded building, a sense of real panic came over him. It was an emotional trauma that would not go away. Professor Drummond wrote of its effects upon him:

> Through the years, whenever a large crowd assembled to hear him, the infamous day would seemingly come forth with fresh vigor to plague his spirit. Even the verse of Scripture from which he preached on that occasion (Proverbs 3:33) revived the depressing memory. He would turn pale on hearing it.[11]

Just eighteen months after the incident, a building collapsed under the weight of snow the morning after Spurgeon had preached there the night before. Spurgeon vowed that if lives again had been lost, he would preach no more. Fortunately, such a thing never occurred.

Mrs. Spurgeon wrote about the effects of the Surrey Music Hall incident upon her husband:

> He carried the scars of that conflict to his dying day, and never afterwards had he the physical vigor and strength which he possessed before passing through that fierce trial. Verily, it was a thorny path by which the Lord led him. Human love would have protected him at any cost from an ordeal so terrible, and suffering so acute; but God's love saw the end from the beginning, and "He never makes a mistake." Though we may not, at the time, see His purpose in the afflictions which He sends us, it will be plainly revealed when the light of eternity falls upon the road along which we have journeyed.[12]

The Burden of Sharing Others' Struggles

Spurgeon also experienced the usual stresses and strains that came from a very busy ministry. In addition to the rigors of weekly sermon preparation were the directing of multiple ministries, the editing/writing deadlines, the many invitations to speak, the care of and provision for his family, and the involvement in many other spheres of the Lord's work. Spurgeon also was given to counseling fellow ministers. The numerous men who came to Spurgeon to pour out their troubles to him also took a heavy toll. Not only did he listen to those who were hurting among his congregation but also many of the men who came out of The Pastors' College sought solace from him. James Douglas, one of his students, said that he saw Spurgeon hearing so many burdens from other men that he determined never to share any personal troubles with him from that time onward. Douglas pledged to share only blessings with him so that he could help to lift his spirits. No doubt, the burdens of other pastors' personal plights shared with Spurgeon laid him low on many occasions. Depression seemed to haunt Spurgeon frequently throughout his ministry.

Spurgeon never doubted the message of the gospel of Christ, but he sometimes doubted himself as the messenger. He reportedly said that he felt more like a waiter at the divine feast of the Master and less a recipient of that which he served to others. Once, when he was extremely low, he traveled out to the countryside for a weekend and attended a small village church. The preacher did not recognize his famous guest and proceeded to deliver a message that was one of Spurgeon's own sermons. Afterward, Spurgeon approached the young pastor, introduced himself to him, and thanked him for his ministry. The pastor turned eight different shades of red as he admitted embarrassingly that he had just preached one of Spurgeon's sermons. Spurgeon replied that he had indeed recognized the sermon but that it was exactly what he needed to hear. He told the startled preacher that through that sermon, God assured him that the message he had preached to others he was able to receive to himself. It was a refreshing and comforting experience in the life of the emotionally distraught pastor.

Spiritual Suffering

Spurgeon believed that spiritual suffering was necessary for the Christian to be in the right position to serve God. He had experienced varying degrees of spiritual anguish, going back to the time before his conversion. From the age of ten to fifteen, he had journeyed on a pilgrimage to faith that included bitter times of facing his plight without Christ. He referred to "the justice of God," which he said,

... like a ploughshare, tore my spirit. I was condemned, undone, destroyed—lost, helpless, hopeless—I thought hell was before me. Then there came a cross-ploughing, for when I went to hear the gospel, it did not comfort me.... The choicest promises of God frowned upon me.... I prayed, but found no answer of peace.[13]

To Spurgeon, no suffering that he later endured could equal this devastating bitterness of soul. These spiritual sufferings taught him to loathe the foulness of sin and to cherish the holiness of God. And they engendered within him a seraphic joy in his salvation. Looking back to his conversion, Spurgeon continued,

> The abundant benefit which we now reap from the deep ploughing of our heart is enough of itself to reconcile us to the severity of the process. Precious is that wine which is pressed in the wine vat of conviction; pure is that gold which is dug from the mines of repentance; and bright are those pearls which are found in the caverns of deep distress.[14]

Spurgeon never lost his innate consciousness of sin and the havoc it could wreak in one's life. He looked back with gratitude upon his conversion and never forgot the horrors of conviction that he felt in his sin.

Spurgeon did not believe, as do some prominent "health-and-wealth" television preachers of today, that suffering ends with salvation. He rejoiced in his sufferings and the way they drove him to depend constantly upon the Lord. He believed that they were part of God's overall purpose for his life:

> The God of providence has limited the time, manner, intensity, repetition, and effects of all our sicknesses; each throb is decreed, each sleepless hour predestinated, each relapse ordained, each depression of spirit foreknown, and each sanctifying result eternally purposed. Nothing great or small escapes the ordaining hand of Him who numbers the hairs of our head.[15]

Even in his darkest hours, Spurgeon was confident that God would see him through with enduring hope for the future:

We may descend in spirit very low till we seem to be plunged in the abyss of hell; but we shall not be left there. We may appear to be at death's door in heart, and soul, and consciousness; but we cannot remain there. Our inward death as to joy and hope may proceed very far; but it cannot run on to its full consequences, so as to reach the utter corruption of black despair. We may go very low, but not lower than the Lord permits; we may stay in the lowest dungeon of doubt for a while, but we shall not perish there. The star of hope is still in the sky when the night is blackest. The Lord will not forget us and hand us over to the enemy. Let us rest in hope. We have to deal with One whose mercy endureth for ever. Surely, out of death, and darkness, and despair we shall yet arise to life, light, and liberty.[16]

The Remedy for Suffering

How did Spurgeon deal with his various sufferings? To rise above his painful situation, he used various means, among them the following.

The Use of Medication

Spurgeon was not one to shy away from using the latest medical treatments available. He consulted physicians and used common remedies of the day for the various maladies he experienced. Although Christians know that the Great Physician can heal any illness supernaturally, we also believe that He works through various means to bring healing. If Spurgeon could gain relief from medical treatments, he was not hesitant to seek them. Christian leaders today should not shun the latest medical treatments, but use them in a holistic approach to receive healing for their lives. Obviously, the dangers of unmerited radical treatments and the danger of abusing prescription drugs should serve as warnings to anyone seeking relief from their ailments.

The Bolstering of Letters

Spurgeon spent a great deal of time writing letters. In fact, one of his biographers noted that he wrote about five hundred letters per week. Granted, the typical letter was one brief page, but, the effort was incredible given his many illnesses. And he did not dictate these letters to a secretary but wrote them by hand with a pen that he had to dip in an ink well several times a minute.

Sometimes, his arthritic hands were so swollen that he wrote these letters in the midst of his own agony. The correspondence seemed to serve as therapy to him in his physical trials because even when he was down in his ailments, he would still send and receive letters of encouragement and ministry. He referred in his letters much to his physical situation, and it is apparent that the effort was cathartic for both him and the saints whom he comforted or the sinners he exhorted to salvation.

The Treatment of Humor

Spurgeon had a great sense of humor. He often spoke of his illness in humorous terms: "I have had sharp pains," he wrote to a friend, "but I am recovering. Only my back is broken, and I need a new vertebrae."[17] William Williams, a fellow pastor who kept company with Spurgeon, was a near and dear friend in the latter years of Spurgeon's life. He wrote,

> What a bubbling fountain of humour Mr. Spurgeon had! I laughed more, I verily believe, when in his company than during all the rest of my life besides. He had the most fascinating gift of laughter . . . and he had also the greatest ability for making all who heard him laugh with him. When someone blamed him for saying humourous things in his sermons, he said, "He would not blame me if he only knew how many of them I keep back."[18]

Once, when Spurgeon was feeling depressed, he spoke of the remedy of laughter:

> The other evening I was riding home after a heavy day's work. I felt wearied and sore depressed, when swiftly and suddenly that text came to me, 'My grace is sufficient for the . . .' I reached home and looked it up in the original, and at last it came to me in this way. 'My grace is sufficient for THEE.' And I said, 'I should think it is, Lord,' and I burst out laughing. I never understood what the holy laughter of Abraham was till then. It seemed to make unbelief so absurd. . . . O brethren, be great believers. Little faith will

bring your souls to heaven, but great faith will bring heaven to your souls.[19]

Spurgeon knew well that "a merry heart doeth good like a medicine" (Prov. 17:22); he used laughter to help soothe his spirits when he was low.

The Remedy of Writing

Undoubtedly, we would not have the body of sermons and other writings of Spurgeon that have ministered to so many people if not for his suffering. Some of Spurgeon's greatest work came from the fires of affliction. When he was suffering from his illnesses or found himself the object of criticism, he wrote inspiring devotions. His devotional books are full of quotations that came from his trials and tribulations. His writing was a diversion from his illness and bouts with depression. Amazingly, he not only preached and edited thousands of sermons but also wrote major works, such as his seven-volume treatise on the Psalms, *The Treasury of David,* plus edited his monthly church newsletter *The Sword and the Trowel.* Writing was a great aid in overcoming his personal pain and suffering, no doubt contributing to the 140 works that he authored.

The Refreshment of Travel

When Spurgeon suffered from various times of illness, he would retreat, most often to Mentone in the south of France, where he could have time to recover. Sometimes the retreats lasted for several months, especially in the wintertime, when the cold and damp of London seemed to wreak its greatest havoc upon his frail system. He would return to his pulpit, often in the spring, refreshed and renewed and with a vigorous response from his loving congregation.

At other times, he would take long journeys to revive his spirit and ease his bouts of depression. He wrote in his *Autobiography,* "Though wearied by the long hours of travelling, I am in every way more fresh and free from depression. May the Lord enrich me also in spiritual blessings, and send me back more capable of serving Him than I have ever been!"[20]

The Therapy of Prayer

Spurgeon was a great believer in prayer. He often praised God and thanked the people in his church for their prevailing prayers, which he believed helped ease his suffering and brought restoration to him. On one occasion, he received a letter, signed by the deacons and elders, that concluded thus:

> And now, beloved Pastor, we leave you, with many prayers, in the hands of your Father and our Father. May He have you in His safe keeping, preserve you from lowness and depression of spirits, cheer you with the light of His countenance, strengthen and sustain you by His gracious Spirit, and, in His own good time, bring you again to your beloved Tabernacle "in the fullness of the blessing of the gospel of Christ." This is our fervent prayer.[21]

In 1871, Spurgeon had a long and painful illness that kept him out of his pulpit for twelve Sundays. He wrote many times to the congregation at the Tabernacle, seeking their prayers:

> Dear Friends, The furnace still blows around me. Since I last preached to you, I have been brought very low. My flesh has been tortured with pain, and my spirit has been prostrate with depression. . . . You do pray for me, I know; but I entreat you not to cease your supplications. I am as a potter's vessel when it is utterly broken, useless, and laid aside. Nights of watching, and days of weeping have been mine, but I hope the cloud is passing. . . . In this relative trial, a very keen one, I again ask your prayers. The Lord be with you evermore! Amen. So prays,—Your suffering Pastor, C.H.S.[22]

Exhorting the Church to Prayer

At one point in his illness, he reproved the church for not gathering for special prayer for his recovery: "Perhaps, if *the church* met for prayer, I should be speedily restored. I know thousands do pray, but should not the church do so *as a church?*"[23] The Pastor's suggestion that the church should meet for prayer was immediately set in motion, and the result was thus chronicled in the next letter:

My Beloved Friends, As soon as the church had resolved to meet for special prayer for me, I began rapidly to recover. . . . We may truthfully say of the Wednesday meeting for prayer, that the Lord fulfilled this Word: "Before they call, I will answer; and while they are yet speaking, I will hear." For all this great goodness, I pray you to unite with me in sincere and intense gratitude to the Lord our God.[24]

The occasion was one of many that the pastor blessed the Lord for the healing power of prayer. Before long, Spurgeon was back in the pulpit, and used his suffering as a means of ministering to others through his proclamation.

Spurgeon's Lack of Physical Attention

I must state that Spurgeon's care, or rather the lack thereof, of his own physical well-being might have contributed to his suffering. He was a habitual smoker, as were many men in his day. He smoked cigars regularly and shared even from the pulpit that they brought him solace in his pain. He also became quite portly and was referred to as "the apostle of roast beef and racy religion."[25] Food might have been a comfort, but Spurgeon's excess weight no doubt exacerbated his physical illnesses. In addition, he did not exercise regularly, with the exception of occasional strolls in the park or infrequent ambles in the countryside.

The ministry can be a very sedentary occupation, and Spurgeon's lack of exercise contributed to his declining health. Today, we have a healthy emphasis on the right diet and physical exercise. All leaders would do well to follow disciplined regimens in these most important areas. Spurgeon's example should be a warning to us all to do everything possible to care for the temple that God has given to us.

The Instruction of Suffering

Spurgeon believed in the school of affliction. He identified with David, whom he said had been "tutored in the best of all schools—the school of heart-felt, personal experience."[26] He believed that it was God's way of preparation for the noblest cause of the gospel: "We have to be cut with the sharp knife of affliction, for only then can the Lord make use of us."[27] Spurgeon believed that affliction was absolutely necessary to keep the minister of God at a point where he could be most effective:

> I am sorry to say that I am made of such ill stuff that my Lord has to chasten me often and sorely. I am like a quill pen that will not write unless it be often nibbed, and therefore I have felt the sharp knife many times; and yet I shall not regret my pains and crosses so long as my Lord will write with me on men's hearts. That is the cause of many ministers' afflictions; they are necessary to our work. You have heard the fable of the raven that wished to drink, but the pitcher had so little water in it that he could not reach it, and therefore he took stone after stone, and dropped them into the vessel until the water rose to the brim, and he could drink. There is so little grace, in some men, that they need many sicknesses, bereavements, and other afflictions to make their graces available for usefulness. If, however, we receive grace enough to bear fruit without continual pruning, so much the better.[28]

Spurgeon knew the sufficient grace of the Lord to bear fruit even in the most dire circumstances of his life.

The Ministry of Suffering

One can lead from strength, and one can lead from weakness. Spurgeon used his illness and shortcomings as a means of identifying with the hurts of his hearers. He had great empathy for their weaknesses. Spurgeon said, "I would go to the deeps a hundred times to cheer a downcast spirit. It is good for me to have been afflicted, that I might know how to speak a word in season to one that is weary."[29]

Spurgeon often mentioned his afflictions in his sermons. He used it as a means to comfort the hurting ones in his congregation. One particular message came from the fires of his own physical suffering. It was delivered at the Surrey Gardens Music Hall on November 7, 1858, when Spurgeon was just twenty-four years old. He spoke of his own torment: "I was lying upon my couch during this last week, and my spirits were sunken so low that I could weep by the hour like a child, and yet I knew not what I wept for."[30] In that message, he used the text from 1 Peter 1:6: "Wherein ye greatly rejoice, though now for a season, if need be, ye are in heaviness through manifold temptations" (KJV).

He shared about the paradox in trials of "heaviness" and "rejoicing." He believed that heaviness was a needful experience for the believer for the following reasons. First, without heaviness we would not be like Jesus, who, before His betrayal and arrest, told His disciples, "My soul is exceeding sorrowful, even unto death" (Matt. 26:38). Second, without heaviness we would become too proud and think too much of ourselves. In our trials, we discover of what we are made and are humbled by our adversities. Third, in heaviness we learn lessons that we could not learn elsewhere. "Men will never become great in divinity until they become great in suffering."[31] Fourth, this heaviness is a necessary experience for the Christian who desires to do good to others. It produces a godly empathy that otherwise would not be possible.

He was convinced that at times in each of our lives heaviness of heart is necessary. But he believed that it was intended only for a season, not for a lifetime. Heaviness that leads to excessive periods of despondency is not productive. Spurgeon said, "Despondency is not a virtue; I believe it is a vice. I am heartily ashamed of myself for falling into it, but I am sure there is no remedy for it like a holy faith in God."[32] Such faith enabled Spurgeon to turn his tremendous trials into useful means for the ministry of the gospel.

An Addendum: "The Minister's Fainting Fits"

Many Christian leaders become discouraged.[33] The work doesn't go as one imagines, the church doesn't grow as one desires, lay leaders won't cooperate with one's leadership, people are excessively critical, or finances are down. The list goes on and on. Someone said that discouragement is the occupational hazard of the ministry, and Spurgeon was no exception to this rule. As successful as he was, he still experienced discouragement, and, in his case, it often deteriorated into depression. He became so depressed at times that he could barely function. In his lecture on "The Minister's Fainting Fits," Spurgeon opened with these words: "As it is recorded that David, in the heat of battle, waxed faint, so may it be written of all the servants of the Lord. Fits of depression come over the most of us. . . . The strong are not always vigorous, the wise not always ready, the brave not always courageous, and the joyous not always happy."[34]

Lessons from "The Minister's Fainting Fits"

Great expectations and demands are upon the typical pastor. I have often stated, sometimes jocularly, to my congregation, "The ministry is one big guilt trip. There is always something I should be doing—a sermon I should be writing, someone I should be visiting, someone who needs my help." If permitted, the pressures of the ministry can exact frustration and even despair.

In his lecture titled "The Minister's Fainting Fits," delivered to his students at The Pastors' College, Spurgeon revealed a great deal about his own psyche and the effects of depression that often beset him in an otherwise illustrious ministry. That lecture is a solace to anyone who has been visited by the doubts, difficulties, and despair that often accompany the great responsibility of Christian leadership. Following are excerpts from that lecture.

> *Fits of depression come over the most of us.* Usually cheerful as we may be, we must at intervals be cast down. The strong are not always vigorous, the wise not always ready, the brave not always courageous, and the joyous not always happy. Instead of multiplying eases, let us dwell upon the reasons why these things are permitted:
>
> Is it not first, *that we are men?* Great men are promised tribulation in this world, and ministers may expect a larger share than others, that they may learn sympathy with the Lord's suffering people, and so may be fitting shepherds of an ailing flock.
>
> Moreover, *most of us are in some way or other unsound physically.* The great mass of us labour under some form or other of infirmity, either in body or mind. These infirmities may be no detriment to a man's career of special usefulness; they may even have been imposed upon him by divine wisdom as necessary qualifications for his peculiar course of service.
>
> *Our work, when earnestly undertaken, lays us open to attacks in the direction of depression.* Who can bear the weight of souls without sometimes sinking to the dust? Passionate longings after men's conversion, if not fully satisfied, consume the soul with anxiety and disappointment. To see the hopeful turn aside, the godly grow cold, professors abusing their privileges, and sinners waxing more bold in sin—are not these sights enough to crush us to the earth?
>
> *Our position in the church will also conduce to this.* A minister

fully equipped for his work, will usually be a spirit by himself, above, beyond, and apart from others. Men of God who rise above their fellows into nearer communion with heavenly things, in their weaker moments feel the lack of human sympathy. This loneliness, which if I mistake not is felt by many of my brethren, is a fertile source of depression. . . .

There can be little doubt that *sedentary habits* have a tendency to create despondency in some constitutions. Burton, in his "Anatomy of Melancholy" says—"Students are negligent of their bodies." To sit long in one posture, poring over a book, or driving a quill, is in itself a taxing of nature; but add to this a badly-ventilated chamber, a body which has long been without muscular exercise, and heart burdened with many cares, and we have all the elements for preparing a seething cauldron of despair. . . .

The times most favorable to fits of depression, so far as I have experienced. First among them, I must mention *the hour of great success.* When at last a long-cherished desire is fulfilled, when God has been glorified greatly by our means, and a great triumph achieved, then we are apt to faint. It might be imagined that amid special favours our soul would soar to heights of ecstasy, and re-joice with joy unspeakable, but it is generally the reverse. Excess of joy or excitement must be paid for by subsequent depressions.

Before any great achievement, some measure of the depression is very usual. Surveying the difficulties before us, our hearts sink within us. Such was my experience when I first became a pastor in Lon-don. My success appalled me; and the thought of the career which it seemed to open up, so far from elating me, cast me into the low-est depth, out of which I uttered my miserere and found no room for a gloria in excelsis.

In the midst of a long stretch of unbroken labour, the same af-fliction may be looked for. The bow cannot be always bent without fear of breaking. Repose is as needful to the mind as sleep to the body. Our Sabbaths are days of toil, and if we do not rest upon some other day we shall break down. Rest time is not waste time. It is economy to gather fresh strength.

One crushing stroke has sometimes laid the minister very low. The brother most relied upon becomes a traitor. Equally overwhelming is the blow when an honoured and beloved member yields to temptation, and disgraces the holy name with which he was named. Strife, also, and division, and slander, and foolish censures, have often laid holy men prostrate, and made them go "as with a sword in their bones." Many of the best of ministers, from the very spirituality of their character, are exceedingly sensitive—too sensitive for such a world as this. The trials of a true minister are not few, and such as are caused by ungrateful professors are harder to bear than the coarsest attacks of avowed enemies.

When troubles multiply, and discouragements follow each other in long succession . . . despondency despoils the heart of all its peace. Constant dropping wears away stones, and the bravest minds feel the fret of repeated afflictions. Accumulated distresses increase each other's weight; they play into each other's hands, and, like bands of robbers, ruthlessly destroy our comfort.

This evil will also come upon us, we know not why, and then it is all the more difficult to drive away. Causeless depression is not to be reasoned with, nor can David's harp charm it away by sweet discoursings. As well fight with the mist as with this shapeless, undefinable, yet all-beclouding hopelessness. One affords himself no pity when in this case, because it seems so unreasonable, and even sinful to be troubled without manifest cause; and yet troubled the man is, even in the very depths of his spirit.

The lesson of wisdom is, *be not dismayed by soul trouble.* Count it no strange thing, but a part of ordinary ministerial experience. Cast the burden of the present, along with the sin of the past and the fear of the future, upon the Lord, who forsaketh not his saints. Continue, with double earnestness to serve your Lord when no visible result is before you. In nothing let us be turned aside from the path which the divine call has urged us to pursue. Come fair or come foul, the pulpit is our watch-tower, and the ministry our warfare; be it ours, when we cannot see the face of our God, to trust under THE SHADOW OF HIS WINGS.[35]

SPURGEON'S LEADERSHIP LESSONS

- **Leadership always comes with a cost.** That cost often takes a toll on the personal well-being of a leader from within. Spurgeon suffered greatly throughout his ministry, especially from rheumatic gout, which led to severe depression and other complications.
- **Depression can afflict even the greatest leader.** Abraham Lincoln, Winston Churchill, and others suffered from depression their entire lives. Spurgeon had long bouts with depression and lamented that "there are dungeons underneath the Castle of Despair."
- **Personal suffering factors into the overall impact that a leader has through his life and ministry.** Suffering had a tremendous impact on the depth and quality of the preaching, writing, and other aspects of Spurgeon's ministry. He wrote, "We have to be cut with the sharp knife of affliction, for only then can the Lord make use of us."
- **Suffering is an integral part to one's spiritual journey.** Spurgeon believed that suffering was a normal part of the Christian life. He agreed with the apostle Paul, who wrote to the Philippian church about "the fellowship of [Christ's] sufferings." Spurgeon wrote that "neither goodness, nor greatness can deliver you from affliction."
- **Prayer is a great remedy for suffering.** Spurgeon was a great believer in prayer. He often praised God and thanked the people in his church for their prevailing prayers, which he believed helped ease his suffering and brought restoration to him.
- **A leader can lead from weakness as well as from strength.** Spurgeon used his illness and shortcomings as a means of identifying with the hurts of his hearers. He said, "I would go to the deeps a hundred times to cheer a downcast spirit. It is good for me to have been afflicted, that I might know how to speak a word in season to one that is weary."
- **A leader should not be overcome by his suffering.** As much as Spurgeon suffered, he was ever confident that there would be a better day. He wrote, "The star of hope is still in the sky when the night is blackest. The Lord will not forget us and hand us over to the enemy. Let us rest in hope. . . . Surely, out of death, and darkness, and despair we shall yet arise to life, light, and liberty.

PART THREE

Applying the Lessons
of a Leader

13

A LEADER FOR
THE WORLD IN CRISIS

*Send down Thy Spirit upon Thy servant, that he, whilst
trembling in weakness, may be made strong to preach Thy
Word, to lead forth this people in holy prayer, and to help them
in that humiliation for which this day is set apart.*[1]

A leader faces many challenges, but perhaps none greater than when one's nation is thrust into a time of crisis. The Bible gives many examples of godly leaders who rose to provide the kind of leadership necessary when their nation faced danger or aggression. Moses responded to God's call, leading the Israelites out of bondage in Egypt and guiding them through the many years of wilderness wandering that followed. He then passed the mantle of leadership to Joshua, who valiantly led his nation to advance, move into, and possess the land God had promised them. David provided strategic leadership in building the nation of Israel, withstanding numerous conflicts from without. Nehemiah exercised excellent leadership when leading the Israelites to return to Jerusalem and rebuild the walls that the Babylonians had destroyed. These men became inspirational models for other leaders who followed in later years.

Throughout history, both secular and religious leaders have been called upon to offer spiritual leadership and consolation in times of national crisis. In America, such secular leadership was personified in President Abraham Lincoln.

"Redeemer President"

Americans faced a devastating war when the North and the South became embroiled in a civil strife that resulted in the deaths of 623,000 soldiers from 1860 to 1865. President Lincoln is remembered most for his brief Gettysburg Address and its "words that remade America."[2] But Allen Guelzo, in his book *Abraham Lincoln: Redeemer President*, contends that Lincoln should be remembered more for his second inaugural address on March 4, 1865. Although Lincoln could have reveled in the victory that the North would soon win, Lincoln chose to use the occasion to reflect on the nation's sin and the judgment of God upon both sides of the conflict. Lincoln sought to initiate a course of leadership that would bind up the nation's wounds, depicted best in the following phrase from the speech: "With malice toward none; with charity for all." His appeal for reconciliation in the nation received a mixed response, but black abolitionist Frederick Douglass commented following the inaugural address, "Mister Lincoln, that was a sacred effort."[3]

Lincoln never had the chance to implement his healing vision for the nation because he was assassinated on April 14, a little more than a month following his second inauguration. But, like leaders before him, Lincoln modeled the distinctive notion that secular leaders can provide spiritual leadership at times of national crisis. In more recent times, we have again seen the need for American leaders to provide spiritual leadership at one of the most horrific moments in our history.

The Attack on America

On September 11, 2001, America was caught off guard in a surprise attack by a group of Islamic terrorists who orchestrated a suicidal mission of unprecedented devastation. A small band of terrorists independently overcame the flight crews of four commercial flights filled with civilian passengers. They transformed the planes into weapons of warfare intended for specific targets. They crashed two of the hijacked planes violently into the Twin Towers of the World Trade Center in New York City. They crashed a third plane into the Pentagon in Washington, D.C. Only one flight failed to reach its destination. A group of heroic passengers prevented the fourth flight from reaching its terrorist target in Washington. Those heroes charged the hijackers and subsequently forced the plane down near Pittsburgh. As the Twin Towers of the

World Trade Center crumbled into an infernal heap, as smoke billowed from the destruction at the nation's military headquarters, and as the crater at the crash sight smoldered in Pennsylvania, the country began to awaken to the horror of the coordinated plot that had wiped out the lives of nearly three thousand innocent citizens.

For the most part, Americans believed that the nation's skies had been secure before 9/11. But the country was suddenly shocked into the reality of the vulnerability of its public air transportation system to such an attack. Nothing close to such an assault within America had occurred since the Japanese launched a surprise air attack on the military bases in Pearl Harbor, ushering America into the Second World War.

The nation reeled, trying to comprehend the devastating nature of such a seemingly senseless act of aggression. President George W. Bush, along with other national leaders, was thrust into an emergency-mode style of leadership, and grappled with the aftermath of grief and fear that gripped much of the nation.

Billy Graham at the National Cathedral

As part of the President's initial response to the attack, he called for a National Day of Prayer and Remembrance. The Rev. Billy Graham, spiritual advisor to many presidents and generally recognized as the Christian statesman for the nation, was asked to lead the special service. Other religious leaders from different faiths were also invited to participate in the unique occasion at the National Cathedral in Washington on September 14, 2001. In his striking address, Graham made the following remarks:

> Today, we especially come together in this service to confess our need of God. We've always needed God from the very beginning of this nation, but today we need Him especially. We're facing a new kind of enemy. We're involved in a new kind of warfare and we need the help of the Spirit of God. The Bible's words are our hope: "God is our refuge and strength, an ever present help in trouble. Therefore we will not fear, though the earth give way and the mountains fall into the heart of the sea." [Ps. 46:1–2 NIV][4]

Graham's comments mirrored statements by a previous spiritual leader who faced a similar challenge during a time of national crisis in Great Britain in 1857. A mutinous uprising had occurred in India, at that time a colony of the British Empire. Many soldiers and British loyalists had lost their lives in the insurrection. As the nation looked for guidance in an effort to respond to the tragedy, they called upon a young pastor who had already proven himself to be a religious leader of national prominence in the heart of London. His name was Charles Haddon Spurgeon.

Spurgeon and the National Fast–Day

C. H. Spurgeon, only twenty-three years old at the time, was asked to preach at a National Day of Humiliation and Prayer Service held at the newly constructed Crystal Palace in London on October 7, 1857. It became the largest assembly of people that he would ever address in an enclosed building. The momentous service was attended by 23,654 people on the day appointed by the proclamation of Queen Victoria "for a solemn fast, humiliation, and prayer before Almighty God: in order to obtain pardon for our sins, and for imploring His blessing and assistance on our arms for the restoration of tranquility in India."[5]

Like Billy Graham and other religious leaders who have been asked to give spiritual guidance for the nation at such times, Spurgeon rose to the occasion in leading his countrymen in a protracted time of prayer. He challenged them to repent and exhorted them to trust God in that time of great national duress. Spurgeon's leadership as exhibited in the solemn service that he conducted on that significant day is instructive for all leaders who might encounter similar situations.

One interesting incident occurred before the service began. Spurgeon, upon mounting the platform, became quite nervous, even more so as he looked out and saw his wife in the crowd. Mrs. Spurgeon, knowing the tremendous pressure that was being put upon her husband must have conveyed some anxiety in her countenance. No doubt, the thousands of people who had come to the service had great expectations. Spurgeon beckoned one of his deacons to come to him and whispered in his ear. The deacon proceeded to go out into the audience to where Mrs. Spurgeon was seated. He told her that her husband had requested that she please relocate to another seat where he could not see her because when he observed her expression, it made him nervous. Mrs. Spurgeon graciously moved to a different location, out of her husband's sight, and the service proceeded.

Seeking God's Help

In times of crisis, a Christian leader to whom people look for guidance must bring people together to seek God's aid and unite their hearts and minds in prayer. When America's tragedy occurred on September 11, 2001, the nation was moved by the leadership of the U.S. Congress who gathered on the steps of the U.S. Capitol the day after the attacks for a special time of prayer. Republicans and Democrats alike became nonpartisan Americans that memorable day, and for some days to follow, as they united in calling upon God in prayer. At the conclusion, they linked arms and sang "God Bless America." Few Americans would forget the tremendous spectacle of atypical unity that was displayed by those elected leaders.

At the beginning of the Fast-Day service on October 7, 1857, Spurgeon led the huge congregation in a time of consecrated prayer, in which he invoked God's help. He prayed for the ones who had suffered through the mutiny, especially the widows and the fatherless. In reference to the soldiers, he prayed that God would "Give strength to our soldiers to execute upon the criminals the sentence which justice dictates; and then, by Thy strong arm, and by Thy terrible might, do Thou prevent a repetition of so fearful an outrage."[6] Spurgeon called for God's assistance in meting out justice to those who had caused the destruction of life, and for His will to be accomplished in the cause before them.

Calling for Repentance

A nation that experiences tragedy may naturally turn toward introspection and self-examination. Christians realize that whereas God might not *cause* such events, in His providence He *allows* them to occur, perhaps for specific reasons. When crisis comes, a nation is compelled to consider its own need for confession of sin. Israel was warned of its need for repentance because of its rebellion against God. God promised healing only if they would respond and repent: "If my people, who are called by my name, will humble themselves and pray and seek my face and turn from their wicked ways, then will I hear from heaven and will forgive their sin and heal their land" (2 Chron. 7:14 NIV).

Christian author Henry Blackaby, speaking to a women's conference sometime later, called the events of September 11 "a horrendous move in the history of our nation." He commented that he believed that in the attacks God was trying to tell His people that He was beginning to remove the hedge of protection from us because of our sins. He further stated that God was holding Christians accountable for making a difference in their world. He urged those in attendance to pray intentionally for revival in America.[7]

Christian leaders are exercising appropriate leadership when they call for repentance, that no obstruction might impede God's hearing and acting upon a nation's request for divine assistance. Indeed, many religious leaders in America heeded the wake-up call for Christians to unite in prayer and repentance for national sins. Pastors and churches all across the nation led the way in seeking God's face through prayer and repentance. In the same way, Spurgeon directed the assembly in the Crystal Palace to seek repentance:

> O Lord, it is ours this day to humble ourselves before Thee. We are a sinful nation; we confess the sins of our governors and our own particular iniquities. For all our rebellions and transgressions, O God have mercy upon us! We plead the blood of Jesus. Help every one of us to repent of sin, to fly to Christ for refuge and grant that each one of us may thus hide ourselves in the rock, till the calamity be overpass, knowing that God will not desert them that put their trust in Jesus.[8]

When a nation is led toward repentance, the door is opened for God to work His healing and restoration as the people turn their hearts toward Him.

Struggling to Understand the Situation

The leader who is thrust into the national spotlight at a time of national crisis bears a grave responsibility. What answers does one give in the face of such dire situations? The task of expressing the feelings of a nation is difficult, to say the least.

Americans struggled to grasp the meaning of the horrific attacks in New York and Washington. Billy Graham stated, "No matter how hard we try, words simply cannot express the horror, the shock, and the revulsion we all feel over what took place in this nation on Tuesday morning. September 11 will go down in our history as a day to remember."[9]

Graham voiced the questions that people were asking and the confusion they were feeling:

But how do we understand something like this? Why does God allow evil like this to take place? Perhaps that is what you are asking now. You may even be angry at God. I want to assure you that God understands these feelings that you may have.[10]

He sought to lead America to know that God cared about what happened in the tragedy of 9/11. He shared valuable lessons from the attacks, reminding us of the mystery and iniquity of evil, the realization that Americans need each other, and that good could still come from such a terrible tragedy.

Spurgeon, likewise, was horrified at the mutinous uprisings and violence in India. He voiced the outrage of the nation and the cry for justice against those who had perpetrated such crimes against humanity. His tone was more militant than that of Graham:

> Look down from heaven, O God, and behold this day the slaughtered thousands of our countrymen. Behold the wives, the daughters of Britain, violated, defiled! Behold her sons, cut in pieces and tormented in a manner which earth hath not beheld before. O God, free us, we beseech Thee, from this awful scourge! Give strength to our soldiers to execute upon the criminals the sentence which justice dictates; and then, by Thy strong arm, and by Thy terrible might, do Thou prevent a repetition of so fearful an outrage.[11]

Not surprisingly, Spurgeon chose as his text Micah 6:9: "Hear ye the rod, and who hath appointed it" (KJV). He spared no words in applying the passage to the situation at hand.

Biographer G. Holden Pike stated that younger generations reading about the incident might not understand "the intensity of feeling which the atrocities of that outbreak aroused."[12] Even some of Spurgeon's contemporaries thought that he was too vindictive in his remarks. But Spurgeon's comments were consistent with his theological belief in a God who brought wrath and judgment upon the peoples who rejected Him. One must understand Spurgeon in the context of the times in which he lived.

Comforting the Hurting

Spiritual leaders in times of national crisis express comfort and compassion to the victims who have suffered greatly. Billy Graham told the national audience that God cared about what happened in America. Already, in those first days before the national prayer service, millions of American citizens had given significant donations for the victims of the attack on September 11. In 1857, Spurgeon led the assembly at the Crystal Palace to demonstrate practical compassion for those who hurt the most by raising funds for the victims of the mutiny in India.

> We pray Thee, remember this day the widow and the fatherless children; think Thou of those who are this day distressed even to the uttermost. Guide the hearts of this great multitude, that they may liberally give and this day bestow of their substance to their poor destitute brethren.[13]

Just as Americans shortly afterwards responded to the needs of the victims and families of the World Trade Center attacks, so the crowd at the Crystal Palace raised a sizeable sum of money to assist the families who had suffered from the Indian mutiny. It was a practical way to show genuine concern for the ones who needed it most.

Providing Hope for the Future

Granted that immediate circumstances after national tragedy can leave citizens feeling a sense of hopelessness, the Christian leader has an obligation before God to point to the hope that lies in Jesus Christ. Billy Graham was adamant in pointing Americans to the future and assuring them of his belief that God would bring healing and restoration from the tragic events that had occurred:

> There's hope for the present because I believe the stage has already been set for a new spirit in our nation. . . . We need a spiritual revival in America. And God has told us in His Word, time after time, that we are to repent of our sins and we're to turn to Him and He will bless us in a new way. . . . But, there is also hope for the future because of God's promises. As a Christian, I have hope, not just for this life, but for heaven and the life to come. And many of those people who died this past week are in heaven right now, and they

wouldn't want to come back. It's so glorious and so wonderful. And that's the hope for all of us who put our faith in God. I pray that you will have this hope in your heart.[14]

Spurgeon, similarly, led the worshipers at the Fast-Day service to look toward God and His hope for them in their situation:

> Our God delights in mercy, and in the deliverance of Britain from its ills. God will be as much pleased as Britain; yea, when Britain shall have forgotten it, and only the page of history shall record his mercies, God will still remember what he did for us in this day of our straits and our difficulties. As to the hope that he will help us it is a certainty. There is no fear that when we unite in prayer God will refuse to hear. It is as sure as that there is a God, that God will hear us; and if we ask him aright, the day shall come when the world shall see what Britain's God has done, and how he has heard her cry, and answered the voice of her supplications.[15]

The responsibility and stress of providing leadership during national crisis can take an emotional toll on the strongest of spiritual leaders. Spurgeon was no exception. Reportedly, he was so exhausted after the Fast-Day service that, when he went to sleep that Wednesday night, he did not awaken until Friday morning. Spurgeon remembered, "It was the only time in my life that I had such an experience. Eternity alone will reveal the full results of the Fast-Day service at the Crystal Palace."[16]

Recovery and Moving Ahead

Britain recovered from its crisis in due course in the mid-1800s, and America recovered to a degree of normalcy in time after 9/11. But things would not be quite the same as they were before. A nation that was once lulled into complacency would be challenged to vigilance in a new era of concern for national security.

Beyond our shores, other nations experienced an escalation of terrorism targeted against their citizens. Wars within the borders of Iraq and Afghanistan signaled global threats that would persist for years to come. Considering the climate of aggression and oppression that persists unabated in many parts of the world, what is the best way for Christian leaders to respond? Politics aside, there are distinct opportunities for Christian leaders to provide courageous leadership and give witness to their faith in the most difficult of times, nationally and internationally.

Regardless of the threats that we may encounter, we can set the example by determinedly moving ahead with our lives, diligently pursuing our life's work, planning for the future, and putting our faith and trust in God. These are not times to be fearful or intimidated by the forces that oppose our mission. We must continue to work for good and accomplish all we can for the kingdom of Jesus Christ. We firmly believe that God is in control. And, ultimately, we entrust our security and our future to His hands. He will not fail us or forsake us.

SPURGEON'S LEADERSHIP LESSONS

- **A nation looks to its leaders for guidance and direction in times of national crisis.** At the young age of twenty-three, Spurgeon was requested to lead a special prayer service for the country in a time of mutinous uprisings in India.
- **A Christian leader to whom people look for guidance must bring people together to seek God's aid and unite their hearts and minds in prayer.** Spurgeon was resolute in leading the country toward worship of God as they sought His divine help and intervention.
- **For a Christian leader to call for national repentance that no obstruction might impede God's granting a nation's request for divine assistance is appropriate.** Spurgeon called on the nation to repent at the same time that he called for divine justice against the perpetrators of violence.
- **In times of national crisis, leaders express comfort and compassion to the victims who have suffered greatly.** Spurgeon led the assembly at the Crystal Palace to demonstrate compassion for the hurting ones by raising funds for the victims of the mutiny in India.
- **The leader who is thrust into the national spotlight at a time of national crisis bears a grave responsibility because people look to him for help in understanding the situation.** Spurgeon voiced the outrage that people were feeling about the murderous insurrection in India, and he promised God's justice according to His Word.
- **In times of national crisis, the Christian leader has an obligation before God to point to the hope that lies in Jesus Christ.** Spurgeon believed that God would continue to bless Britain as she looked to Him for her guidance and direction.

14

A LEADER FOR
THE DAILY CHALLENGE

*In this age, when crowds follow their leaders, and bold men
easily command a following . . . and rough independence
is rarely to be found, it is well for us to be self-contained,
whole men, and not merely limbs of a body, maintaining
ourselves in the integrity of personal thought,
conscience, manner, and action.*[1]

As many styles of leadership might exist as there are leaders. Effective leaders are not limited to any one style or philosophy. Both Robert E. Lee and Ulysses S. Grant, for example, were effective leaders during the Civil War, but they were as different as night and day in personality and style of leadership. Grant graduated near the bottom of his class at West Point whereas Lee graduated near the top. Grant was considered rough, uncouth, and undisciplined in his personal behavior and used the advantage of massive resources to achieve his military goals. Lee, on the other hand, was recognized as a Southern gentle- man—courteous, mannerly, and erudite—and, even with limited men and supplies, he proved prudently resourceful in his battlefield strategies. Grant and Lee were on opposite sides of the national struggle. But they both led successful campaigns and were held in high esteem by their soldiers. Most historians regard them both as effective leaders in their respective roles.

Leadership styles today are as varied as they were in years past. In the busi- ness world, you have the same garden variety of leaders that you would have in any other realm, including the church. Although distinctions exist between Christian and secular leadership, they have similarities in their approaches because, regardless of the type of organization, one is still dealing with people. That common denominator gives a basis for comparing styles of leadership that work.

Typically, four styles of leadership with certain variations are recognized, although they might differ in designation. In their much-acclaimed book *The Leader's Window: Mastering the Four Styles of Leadership to Build High-Performing Teams,* John Beck and Neil Yeager label those four styles as follows: directing, problem-solving, developing, and delegating.[2]

- Style 1 is DIRECTING, or telling employees what to do, when to do it, and how to do it. In its negative form it is called *dominating.* This style is typically associated with *authoritarian* leaders.
- Style 2 is PROBLEM-SOLVING and involves getting together with the employees and listening to their ideas before coming to a decision. Its negative form is *overinvolving* the employees rather than making a decision and getting on with the task at hand—a kind of group wallow. This style is a *consensus* approach to leadership.
- Style 3 is DEVELOPING. The leader acts as a supporter and encourager of the employee as he or she solves any problems. In its negative form it is *overaccommodating.* The leader just lets the employee flounder around without stepping in. This style is a *passive* approach to leadership.
- Style 4 is DELEGATING. The leader assumes that the employee knows what to do and is doing it without the need for direction. In its negative form the leader is *abdicating*, assuming that the task is being carried out. This style is a *detached* approach to leadership.

Beck and Yeager assess the different styles and how leader need to combine the four styles to provide effective leadership. With the help of dozens of real-life case studies and profiles of a number of great political and business leaders, the authors analyze each style for its relative merits in various work situations. And they demonstrate how to master all four styles and to deploy them according to not only the changing needs of the team and the individuals in it but also the ever-changing demands of the marketplace.

The book emphasizes the importance of a leader's using all four styles. One trap into which leaders fall is the 1–4–1 combination of styles in which the leader tells the employee what to do (1); the leader leaves the employee alone (4); and then the leader sees that the employee isn't doing the task the way he expected, so the leader goes back into the directing mode (1). The most useful combination is 1–4–3–2 in which the leader gives direction (1); lets the employee get on with the task (4); meets with the employee to assist with any problems (3); and then, when the employee meets a roadblock, the leader listens

S3—Developing	S2—Problem-solving
• High support—Low direction • Team member decides with direction • Active listening—Limited influencing	• High support—High direction • Leader decides with input • Active listening—Active influencing
S4—Delegating	S1—Directing
• Low support—Low direction • Team member decides alone • Limited listening—Limited influencing	• Low support—High direction • Leader decides alone • Limited listening—Active influencing

Beck and Yeager then give examples of top leaders of industry who use each of these styles as their main way of leading. Also of interest are the examples they give of politicians who use these styles.

Style	Leader	Politics
Style 1	Ray Kroc—McDonald's	Al Gore
Style 2	Bill Gates—Microsoft	George Bush Sr.
Style 3	Jack Welch—General Electric	Corazon Aquino—Philippines
Style 4	Ted Turner—CNN	Ronald Reagan/ George W. Bush

and then makes a decision (2). The book concludes by looking at how to make a group of people a team using the four styles of leadership.

C. H. Spurgeon was a leader who combined the different styles of leadership successfully. As the founder of many benevolent institutions and ministries, he began by exercising the *directing* style of leadership with his organizations, especially in the initial phases of each new work. But then he became a *delegator* in relinquishing direction of the ministry to capable managers and lay leaders. In his involvement in various controversies and taking stands for righteousness, Spurgeon seemed to be running the show. He was the point man who led forth in many of these causes, and others followed suit. He used the "bully pulpit" on many occasions to advance his efforts and persuade others to action.

Some of Spurgeon's style of leadership was dictated by necessity rather than intention. Because of Spurgeon's chronic bouts with rheumatic gout and related illnesses, his absence from his pulpit in London meant that he had to release control of his ministries to his brother, James, and relinquish most important administrative decisions to the various heads of each organization, society, or institution. In addition, the elders assisted his brother in conducting the regular ministries at the Metropolitan Tabernacle. Spurgeon's direction was, of necessity, from the distant vantage at Mentone, where he retreated for physical recovery.

Spurgeon's influence was such that, if he ever had any questions or indicated that changes needed to be made, his wishes were carried out to the best of his subordinates' abilities. The "Guv'nor" was the unquestioned head of the church and its extended ministries. But in his extended absences, Spurgeon needed to know that he could count on his leaders. So it was of utmost importance to him that his leaders had complementary skills, similar beliefs and convictions, and the common purpose of advancing the kingdom of Christ. Although Spurgeon typically employed the *directive* style of leadership, he was not one to lord over others or demand his way. He took seriously the words of Jesus when He called his disciples together and instructed them:

> Jesus called them together and said, "You know that the rulers of the Gentiles *lord it over them,* and their high officials exercise authority over them. Not so with you. Instead, whoever wants to become great among you *must be your servant,* and whoever wants to be first must be your slave—just as the Son of Man did not come to

be served, but to serve, and to give his life as a ransom for many."
(Matt. 20:25–28 NIV, emphasis added)

Earlier, in chapter ten, "Compassion," we devoted significant discussion to
"servant leadership." With certainty, one may state that that designation, more
than any other, describes Spurgeon's style of leadership. He was not interested
in power and control over people. He told his students at The Pastors' College,
"I would sooner be the leader of six free men, whose enthusiastic love is my
only power over them, than play the dictator to a score of enslaved nations."[3]
Spurgeon's mindset was one of service, what he could do to serve both His
Lord and the people.

Leadership is the process of influencing an organized group toward a common goal. It might sound easy, but the practical application can provide a real
challenge. Effective leadership depends on positive, skilled leaders who are able
to lead at different levels. No single leadership style is appropriate in every
situation; therefore, to be an effective leader, you must learn to understand
your environment, situation, and circumstances to help you act accordingly.
Remember, your success as a leader will depend on your assessment of the
situation and your ability to communicate what you want such that others
will desire to fulfill your wishes. That is the art of leadership.

Your goal as a leader is to do the best job you can to influence your people
toward shared goals. Because you are dealing with a diverse group of people, it is
important to understand the different approaches toward motivating them to
meet their goals. Over the years, numerous models have been developed to analyze the different styles of leadership. The best model for you will integrate your
style of leadership with the situation and the development of the follower. Such
a straightforward approach provides an excellent model for leadership.

Assessing someone's leadership style is harder than it at first seems. Leaders
are complex and varied in their personalities, styles, and methods. Most people
try to understand leadership in simple ways rather than in complex ways. Most
leaders lead 80 percent instinctively and 20 percent intentionally (or con-
sciously). This is why many leaders have trouble describing or even understanding their own leadership style.

Every person has a leadership style and will use that style most of the time
when he or she is put into a leadership role. A lot of good analytical tools are
available to help us reflect on our own style. Generally, the more we learn
about our style and reflect on its effectiveness, the better we get at using it.

Also, the more we learn, the more alternatives and options we gain. The more we lead, the more instinctively we are inclined to lead when the occasion arises.

More than anything else, as Christians, we have the confidence of the leadership of the Holy Spirit as we implement different approaches to leading. As we are sensitive to the Spirit's leading, we can, like C. H. Spurgeon, have confidence that the Lord will lead us in the right direction.

Postscript

SPURGEON'S LASTING LEGACY OF LEADERSHIP

You and I might never rise to the level of leadership exemplified by someone such as C. H. Spurgeon. Indeed, relatively few leaders experience the degree of influence and status of a Spurgeon. Those choice servants seem to come along once in a generation, raised up by God for specific purposes that He has ordained in His providence. In the subjective assessment by which we and the world measure our accomplishments, we might think that we could never achieve such a standard of leadership. I trust that you, after having read *Spurgeon on Leadership,* do not think that way.

My intention in writing this book was to use C. H. Spurgeon as a leadership model to inspire and motivate you to achieve every purpose under heaven that God has intended for you to achieve. Observing carefully the way in which God used Spurgeon has great merit, helping us glean spiritual insights that will benefit and help us improve our own leadership potential. In a real sense, that's what this book is about. We can look at what Spurgeon achieved as a leader, heed the divine wisdom that he shared through his writings, and then apply those lessons where appropriate to the circumstances of our own situation. Hopefully, we can make some adjustments that will move us in a positive direction and toward our goal. In the process, we must pray unceasingly that God's timeless leadership principles will take root in our lives and bear fruit for Him. We simply offer our best to the Lord, consistently and wholeheartedly, and then we trust Him for the results.

Regardless of the measure of recognition that comes our way, be assured that each of us has a specific role to play in God's kingdom work on this earth. Our influence might not immediately extend as far as reaching millions of people, but it will affect directly those to whom we are responsible as leaders. They, in turn, will influence the lives of others. Only the Lord knows how those humble beginnings within our circle of influence may in time touch untold numbers of people for the cause of Christ. The important thing is for each one of us to be found faithful in the task to which God has called us and to keep the focus on doing all for His, not our, glory.

God has called us! That fact is remarkable in itself. He counts us worthy and entrusts precious souls to our care. He has a specific purpose for us that He reveals in time. Nothing is more exciting than discovering the manner in which God's divine plan unfolds in our lives! The legacy of Spurgeon shows that God can use any person anywhere if he or she has given himself or herself totally to His service. Never underestimate what God can do through you if you are completely yielded to Him. I pray that the Lord Jesus will bless you richly in your leadership venture and inspire you to develop, grow, and mature into the godly vessel He is shaping you to become.

One day, when we gather around our Lord's throne to worship Him in heaven, we will understand the significance of our earthly achievements in the context of Christ's eternal glory. Our immediate response will be to lay our earthly crowns at the feet of our King as an expression of our grateful love and devotion. Then we will begin to enjoy the heavenly feast of His never-ending presence and the blessing of one another's fellowship forever. Enjoy the journey! The best is yet to come!

Appendix

CHARLES HADDON SPURGEON BIOGRAPHICAL SKETCH

June 19, 1834—Born at Kelvedon, County of Essex, England

January 6, 1850—Spiritual conversion, Colchester

May 3, 1850—Joined Baptist church (Baptized in the River Lark at Isleham)

1850—Preached first sermon, at a Cottage in Teversham

October 12, 1851—Preached first sermon at Waterbeach Baptist Chapel

October 12, 1853—Preached first sermon in London, New Park Street Church

April 28, 1854—Called to pastorate, New Park Street Church (232 members)

January 10, 1855—First sermon published in the "New Park Street Pulpit"

January 8, 1856—Marriage to Susannah Thompson (born 1/15/1832)

September 20, 1856—Twin sons, Thomas and Charles, born

1856—Established The Pastors' College

1857—Preached to largest indoor crowd of 23,654, National Day of Humiliation/ Prayer

March 18, 1861—Opening of new Metropolitan Tabernacle

1864—Initiated Baptismal Regeneration Controversy

1867—Stockwell Orphanage founded

1875—Mrs. Spurgeon inaugurated Book Fund

1887—Downgrade Controversy commenced with articles published in *The Sword and the Trowel*

1888—Spurgeon's mother ELIZA died, aged 75 years

June 7, 1891—Last sermon delivered at Metropolitan Tabernacle

—During his pastorate, 14,692 were baptized and joined the Tabernacle

—As year 1891 ended, membership given as 5,311 (Tabernacle capacity: 6,000, with 5,500 seated, 500 standing room)

January 31, 1892—Died after extended illness, at Mentone, aged 57 years

February 11, 1892—Buried at Norwood Cemetery, London

March 22, 1899—His brother (& Assistant Pastor, Metropolitan Tabernacle) JAMES died, aged 61 years

June 14, 1902—His father (& Pastor) JOHN died, aged almost 92 years

October 22, 1903—His wife (& colaborer) SUSANNAH died, aged 71 years

October 17, 1917—His son (& Pastor) THOMAS died, aged 61 years

December 13, 1926—His son (& Pastor) CHARLES died, aged 70 years

Those persons seeking additional information on Spurgeon,
or desiring to contact the author personally, may do so at
larryjmichael@kregel.com.

ENDNOTES

Introduction

1. James McGregor Burns, *Leadership* (New York: Harper & Row, 1978).

Chapter 1: Competence

1. C. H. Spurgeon, *Lectures to My Students*, 3 vols. (reprint, Grand Rapids: Associated Publishers, 1971), 2:23.
2. C. H. Spurgeon, *C. H. Spurgeon's Autobiography*, vol. 2, *The Early Years (1834–1859)* (Carlisle, Pa.: Banner of Truth Trust, n.d.), 1:207–8.
3. Ibid., 210.
4. Leroy Eims, *Be a Motivational Leader* (Colorado Springs, Colo.: Victor, 1996), 109.
5. C. H. Spurgeon, *An All-Round Ministry* (Pasadena, Tex.: Pilgrim, 1973), 262.
6. John Maxwell, interview, *Growing Churches*, fall 1995: 5.
7. Spurgeon, *Lectures to My Students*, 2:23–38.
8. Spurgeon, *An All-Round Ministry*, 262.
9. Kenneth O. Gangel, *Feeding and Leading* (Wheaton, Ill.: Scripture Press, 1989), 217–20.
10. Ibid.
11. Spurgeon, *Lectures to My Students*, 2:28.
12. Ibid.
13. Ibid.
14. Ibid., 29.
15. Ibid.
16. Ibid.
17. Ibid., 30.
18. John Maxwell, *Developing the Leader Within You* (Nashville: Thomas Nelson, 1993), 201.
19. Spurgeon, *An All-Round Ministry*, 201.
20. Ibid., 254.

21. John le Carré, *The Honourable Schoolboy* (New York: Alfred A. Knopf, 1977), 84.
22. Spurgeon, *An All-Round Ministry*, 267.
23. Ibid., 188.
24. Ibid., 272.
25. Ibid., 267.
26. Ibid., 236.
27. Ibid., 299.
28. Ibid., 237.
29. Ibid., 55.
30. John Maxwell, *Leadership 101* (Nashville: Thomas Nelson, 2002), 75.

Chapter 2: Confidence

1. C. H. Spurgeon, *An All-Round Ministry* (Pasadena, Tex.: Pilgrim, 1973), 184.
2. C. H. Spurgeon, *C. H. Spurgeon's Autobiography* (Albany, Ore.: Ages Digital Library, 1999), 1:120.
3. Ibid., 1:263.
4. Ibid., 1:13.
5. Spurgeon, *An All-Round Ministry*, 184.
6. Spurgeon, *C. H. Spurgeon's Autobiography*, 1:298.
7. Spurgeon, *An All-Round Ministry*, 186.
8. Ibid., 183.
9. Spurgeon, *C. H. Spurgeon's Autobiography*, 2:212.
10. John Maxwell, *Developing the Leader Within You* (Nashville: Thomas Nelson, 1993), 98.
11. John Maxwell, *Leadership 101* (Nashville: Thomas Nelson, 2002), 90.
12. Spurgeon, *An All-Round Ministry*, 18.
13. Spurgeon, *C. H. Spurgeon's Autobiography*, 1:271.
14. Ibid., 2:70
15. Spurgeon, *An All-Round Ministry*, 185.
16. Maxwell, *Developing the Leader*, 84.
17. Spurgeon, *An All-Round Ministry*, 185.
18. Ibid., 303.
19. Peter Wagner, *Leading Your Church to Growth* (Ventura, Calif.: Regal, 1984), 130.
20. Spurgeon, *An All-Round Ministry*, 393.

21. Ibid., 147.

22. Spurgeon, *C. H. Spurgeon's Autobiography,* 1:263.

23. Ibid., 1:186.

24. Spurgeon, *An All-Round Ministry,* 62.

25. Spurgeon, *C. H. Spurgeon's Autobiography,* 1:263.

26. C. H. Spurgeon, *Lectures to My Students,* 3 vols. (reprint, Grand Rapids: Associated Publishers, 1971), 3:161.

27. Os Guiness, *Dining with the Devil* (Grand Rapids: Baker, 1993), 29.

28. Spurgeon, *An All-Round Ministry,* 184.

Chapter 3: Context

1. C. H. Spurgeon, review of "Victoria: Queen and Empress—A Jubilee Memoir," *The Sword and the Trowel* (1887), 23: 290.

2. L. E. Elliott-Binns, *Religion in the Victorian Era* (London: Butterworth, 1953), 8.

3. Horton Davies, *Worship and Theology in England, 1850–1900* (Princeton: Princeton University Press, 1962), 4:173.

4. Elliott-Binns, *Religion in the Victorian Era,* 461.

5. Stephen Neill, *A History of Christian Missions* (Baltimore: Penguin, 1964), 396.

6. Elliott-Binns, *Religion in the Victorian Era,* 483.

7. George W. Truett, "C. H. Spurgeon Centenary," *George W. Truett Library* (Nashville: Broadman, 1980), 3:156.

Chapter 4: Calling

1. C. H. Spurgeon, *An All-Round Ministry* (Pasadena, Tex.: Pilgrim, 1973), 179.

2. C. H. Spurgeon, *C. H. Spurgeon's Autobiography* vol. 2, *The Early Years (1834–1859)* (Carlisle, Pa.: Banner of Truth Trust, n.d.), 1:38.

3. Ibid., 43.

4. Ibid., 88.

5. Ibid.

6. Ibid., 148.

7. Ibid., 163.

8. Ibid., 197.

9. Ibid.

10. C. H. Spurgeon, *Lectures to My Students: A Selection from Addresses*

Delivered to the Students of The Pastors' College, Metropolitan Tabernacle (London: Passmore and Alabaster, n.d.), 1:3.

11. Spurgeon, *An All-Round Ministry,* 64.
12. Ibid., 178.
13. Ibid., 233.
14. C. H. Spurgeon, *Lectures to My Students,* 3 vols. (reprint, Grand Rapids: Associated Publishers, 1971), 1:25.
15. Ibid., 23–30.
16. Ibid., 39.
17. Ibid., 35.
18. Ibid., 37.
19. Spurgeon, *An All-Round Ministry,* 178.
20. Ibid., 197.
21. Ibid.
22. Ibid., 303.
23. Spurgeon, *Lectures to My Students,* 1:8.
24. Spurgeon, *An All-Round Ministry,* 351.
25. Ibid., 249.
26. Ibid., 302.
27. Ibid., 262.
28. Ibid.
29. Ibid., 313.
30. Peter Wagner, *Church Planting for a Greater Harvest* (Ventura, Calif.: Regal, 1990), 46.
31. Spurgeon, *An All-Round Ministry,* 314.
32. Thom Rainer, *Eating the Elephant* (Nashville: Broadman, 1994), 23.
33. Spurgeon, *An All-Round Ministry,* 179.
34. Ibid., 183.
35. Excerpted from manual by Elmer Towns, *Spiritual Church Growth* (Lynchburg, Va.: Church Growth Institute).
36. Spurgeon, *An All-Round Ministry,* 186.
37. Ibid.
38. Gene Getz, "Becoming a Spiritually Mature Leader," in *Leaders on Leadership,* ed. George Barna (Ventura, Calif.: Regal, 1997), 88.
39. Spurgeon, *An All-Round Ministry,* 304.
40. Ibid., 185.
41. Ibid., 342.

Endnotes — 225

42. Ibid., 343.
43. Ibid., 135.
44. Ibid., 306.
45. Ibid., 306–7.
46. Ibid., 307.
47. Ibid., 177.

Chapter 5: Character

1. C. H. Spurgeon, *An All-Round Ministry* (Pasadena, Tex.: Pilgrim, 1973), 245.
2. Cited by Arnold Dallimore, *C. H. Spurgeon* (Chicago: Moody, 1984), 176.
3. *Leadership as a Lifestyle* (Provo, Utah: Executive Excellence, 2001), 2001.
4. Warren Bennis, "Lessons in Leadership from Superconsultant Warren Bennis," interview, *Bottom Line Personal* 17, no. 13 (1 July 1996): 13–14.
5. Extensive treatment is given to this early controversy in the author's doctoral dissertation, "The Effects of Controversy on the Evangelistic Ministry of C. H. Spurgeon" (Southern Baptist Theological Seminary, 1989), 107–28.
6. Jack Hayford, "The Character of a Leader," in *Leaders on Leadership*, ed. George Barna (Ventura, Calif.: Regal, 1997), 79.
7. James Douglas, *The Prince of Preachers* (London: Morgan and Scott, n.d.), chap. 4.
8. Spurgeon, *An All-Round Ministry*, 245.
9. Ibid., 191.
10. C. H. Spurgeon, *Lectures to My Students*, 3 vols. (reprint, Grand Rapids: Associated Publishers, 1971), 1:9.
11. Spurgeon, *An All-Round Ministry*, 46.
12. Spurgeon, *Lectures to My Students*, 1:10.
13. *Holiness* (Darlington, England: Evangelical Press, 2001). Introduction.
14. Spurgeon, *An All-Round Ministry*, 245.
15. Andrew Buchanan, "Jackson Pledges to Continue Work," Associated Press, 22 January 2001.
16. Spurgeon, *An All-Round Ministry*, 137.
17. Spurgeon, *Lectures to My Students*, 1:9.
18. C. B. Hogue, "Spiritual Leadership," *Growing Churches* (spring 1995): 8.

19. Kenneth O. Gangel, *Feeding and Leading* (Wheaton, Ill.: Victor, 1989), 34.
20. Lowell "Bud" Paxson, *Threading the Needle* (New York: HarperCollins, 1998), 148.
21. Spurgeon, *An All-Round Ministry,* 48.
22. C. H. Spurgeon, "The Broken Fence," in *Metropolitan Tabernacle Pulpit,* vol. 59 (London: Passmore & Alabaster, 1913).
23. Ted W. Engstrom and Edward R. Dayton, "Integrity," *Christian Leadership Letter* (August 1983): 3.
24. Spurgeon, *Lectures to My Students,* 1:8.
25. Spurgeon, *An All-Round Ministry,* 137.

Chapter 6: Casting Vision

1. C. H. Spurgeon, *An All-Round Ministry* (Pasadena, Tex.: Pilgrim, 1973), 111.
2. Ed Young Sr., quoted in *Leaders on Leadership,* ed. George Barna (Ventura, Calif.: Regal, 1997), 268.
3. Towns, Elmer. *An Inside Look at Ten of Today's Most Innovative Churches* (Ventura, Calif.: Regal Books, 1990), 135–47.
4. Ed Young, "Increasing Your Creativity Quotient," *Leadership Journal* 21, no. 4 (fall 2000), 79.
5. John Maxwell, *Leadership 101* (Old Tappan, N.J.: Revell, 1991), 105.
6. Ibid., 130
7. Leroy Eims, quoted in George Barna, ed. *Leaders on Leadership* (Ventura, Calif: Regal, 1998), 270.
8. George Barna, ed. *Leaders on Leadership,* 47.
9. Spurgeon, *Lectures to My Students,* 3 vols. (reprint, Grand Rapids: Associated Publishers, 1971), 3:40.
10. John F. Kennedy, speech delivered at Rice University, Houston, Texas, 12 September 1962.
11. Warren Bennis and Burt Nanus, *Leaders* (San Francisco: Harper & Row, 1985), 154.
12. C. H. Spurgeon, *C. H. Spurgeon's Autobiography* (Carlisle, Pa.: Banner of Truth Trust, n.d.), 1:388.
13. Spurgeon, *An All-Round Ministry,* 18–19.
14. Rick Warren, *The Purpose-Driven Church* (Grand Rapids: Zondervan, 1995), 345.
15. Lewis Drummond, *Spurgeon: Prince of Preachers* (Grand Rapids: Kregel, 1992), 8.

16. C. H. Spurgeon, *Morning and Evening* (Albany, Ore.: Ages Digital Library, 1999), 59.

17. Spurgeon, *C. H. Spurgeon's Autobiography*, 2:13–14.

18. Ibid., 13.

19. Leroy Eims, *Be a Motivational Leader* (Colorado Springs, Colo.: Victor, 1996), 80–81.

20. Peter Wagner, *Leading Your Church to Growth* (Glendale, Calif.: Regal, 1984), 186.

21. Spurgeon, *An All-Round Ministry*, 5–6.

22. Ibid., 5.

23. Peter Wagner, *Strategies for Church Growth* (Glendale, Calif.: Regal, 1987), 32–34.

24. Spurgeon, *An All-Round Ministry*, 186.

25. Spurgeon, *Morning and Evening*, 59.

Chapter 7: Courage

1. C. H. Spurgeon, *An All-Round Ministry* (Pasadena, Tex.: Pilgrim, 1973), 37.

2. George Barna, ed., *Leaders on Leadership* (Ventura, Calif.: Regal, 1998), 27.

3. *Reader's Digest,* July 1964. See http://www.conservativeforum.org.

4. John Maxwell, *21 Indispensable Qualities of a Leader* (Nashville: Thomas Nelson, 1999), 43.

5. Spurgeon, *An All-Round Ministry*, 277.

6. C. H. Spurgeon, "Let Us Go Forth" *Metropolitan Tabernacle Pulpit* (London: Passmore & Alabaster, 1871), 10:372.

7. Spurgeon, *An All-Round Ministry*, 34.

8. Ibid., 271–72.

9. Ibid., 273.

10. Ibid., 38.

11. Ibid., 300.

12. Lewis Drummond, *Spurgeon: Prince of Preachers* (Grand Rapids: Kregel, 1992), 611.

13. John C. Carlile, *C. H. Spurgeon: An Interpretive Biography* (London: Religious Tract Society, 1933), 148–49.

14. Spurgeon, *An All-Round Ministry*, 35–36.

15. Clifford Hill, *Blessing the Church?* (Glasgow: HarperCollins, 1995), 227.

16. Spurgeon, *An All-Round Ministry,* 37.
17. C. H. Spurgeon, *The Sword and the Trowel* (1877), 13:195–96.
18. Spurgeon, *An All-Round Ministry,* 308.
19. Eric W. Hayden, *Letting the Lion Loose: C. H. Spurgeon and the Bible* (Belfast: Ambassador Productions, 1984), quoted in British Broadcasting Company television film, "The Calling of C. H. Spurgeon."
20. Spurgeon, *An All-Round Ministry,* 110.
21. C. H. Spurgeon, *The Sword and the Trowel* (1867), 3:43.
22. Eric W. Hayden, *The Unforgettable Spurgeon* (Greenville, S.C.: Emerald House Group, 1997), 113.
23. Cited by James T. Allen, *Life Story of C. H. Spurgeon* (Albany, Ore.: Ages Digital Library, 1999), 17.
24. George Barna, *What Americans Believe* (Ventura, Calif.: Regal, 1991), 292.
25. Os Guinness, *Dining with the Devil* (Grand Rapids: Baker, 1993), 28.
26. Gene Mims, *Kingdom Principles for Church Growth* (Nashville: Convention Press, 1994), 88.
27. Spurgeon, *An All-Round Ministry,* 300.
28. Ibid., 376.
29. Ibid., 380.
30. Ibid., 312.
31. Ibid., 390–91.
32. Spurgeon, "The Beloved Pastor's Plea for Unity," *Metropolitan Tabernacle Pulpit,* 39:512.

Chapter 8: Commitment

1. Spurgeon, *Lectures to My Students,* 3 vols. (reprint, Grand Rapids: Associated Publishers, 1971), 3:17.
2. C. H. Spurgeon, personal diary, June 1850, in *C. H. Spurgeon's Autobiography* (Albany, Ore.: Ages Digital Library, 1999), 1:142.
3. Spurgeon, *Lectures to My Students,* 2:182–83.
4. Eugene B. Habecker, *Rediscovering the Soul of Leadership* (Wheaton, Ill.: Victor, 1996), 48–53.
5. Spurgeon, *C. H. Spurgeon's Autobiography,* 1:20.
6. Ibid., 11.
7. Ibid., 11–12.
8. Spurgeon, *Lectures to My Students,* 1:185.
9. Ibid., 2:72.

10. Ibid., 3:17.
11. Arnold Dallimore, *C. H. Spurgeon* (Chicago: Moody, 1984), 121.
12. Spurgeon, *C. H. Spurgeon's Autobiography,* 4:66.
13. Ibid.
14. Spurgeon, *Lectures to My Students,* 2:57.
15. Spurgeon, *C. H. Spurgeon's Autobiography,* 3:251–52.
16. Ibid., 4:4.
17. Ibid.
18. Ibid., 4:6.
19. Habecker, *Rediscovering the Soul of Leadership,* 53–57.
20. C. H. Spurgeon, *An All-Round Ministry* (Pasadena, Tex.: Pilgrim, 1973), 240.
21. Ibid., 239–46.
22. Spurgeon, *C. H. Spurgeon's Autobiography,* 3:247.
23. Ibid., 257.
24. Ibid., 36.
25. Ibid., 208.
26. Ibid., 112–13.
27. Ibid., 2:21.
28. Ibid., 187.
29. Ibid., 3:276–77.
30. Charles Ray, *Mrs. C. H. Spurgeon* (London: Passmore & Alabaster, 1903), 123.
31. Spurgeon, *C. H. Spurgeon's Autobiography,* 3:156.
32. Burley A. Cunningham, *Spurgeon and His Friendships* (London: Epworth, 1933), 106.
33. Spurgeon, *An All-Round Ministry,* prefatory n. 1.
34. Ibid., 108.

Chapter 9: Creativity

1. Cited by John C. Carlile, *C. H. Spurgeon: An Interpretive Biography* (London: Religious Tract Society, 1933), 111.
2. C. H. Spurgeon, *An All-Round Ministry* (Albany, Ore.: Ages Digital Library, 1999), 17.
3. Ibid.
4. C. H. Spurgeon, *C. H. Spurgeon's Autobiography* (Albany, Ore.: Ages Digital Library, 1999), 1:355.

5. C. H. Spurgeon, *Only a Prayer Meeting* (London: Passmore & Alabaster, 1901), 351.

6. Lewis Drummond, *Spurgeon: Prince of Preachers* (Grand Rapids: Kregel, 1992), 211.

7. Charles Ray, *The Life of Charles Haddon Spurgeon* (London: Passmore & Alabaster, 1903), 195.

8. W. Y. Fullerton, *Charles H. Spurgeon, London's Most Popular Preacher* (Chicago: Moody, 1966), 62.

9. Anonymous, *Charles Haddon Spurgeon: A Biographical Sketch and Appreciation by One Who Knew Him Well* (London: Andrew Melrose, 1903), 101.

10. Ibid., 104.

11. Anonymous, *Pulpit Photography, C. H. Spurgeon* (London: Richard D. Dickinson, 1876), 577.

12. *Spurgeon Pamphlets,* vol. 6, no. 12.

13. *The Freeman,* 12 December 1878.

14. Drummond, *Spurgeon: Prince of Preachers,* 195.

15. *British Standard,* 9 January 1857.

16. J. B. Weatherspoon, "Charles Haddon Spurgeon," *The Review and Expositor* 31 (1934): 411.

17. Ray, *The Life of Charles Haddon Spurgeon,* 196.

18. W. Y. Fullerton, *C. H. Spurgeon: An Interpretive Biography* (London: Religious Tract Society, 1933), 71.

19. G. Holden Pike, *The Life and Work of Charles Haddon Spurgeon* (London: Cassell & Co., n.d.), 380–81.

20. Ibid. 380.

21. Spurgeon, *C. H. Spurgeon's Autobiography,* 2:224.

22. Drummond, *Spurgeon: Prince of Preachers,* 307.

23. C. H. Spurgeon, *Around the Wicket Gate* (Albany, Ore.: Ages Digital Library, 1999), 18.

24. Arnold Dallimore, *C. H. Spurgeon* (Chicago: Moody, 1984), 114.

25. Spurgeon, *C. H. Spurgeon's Autobiography,* 3:109–10.

26. C. H. Spurgeon, *Lectures to My Students,* 3 vols. (reprint, Grand Rapids: Associated Publishers, 1971), 1:vi.

27. Ibid., 151.

28. Spurgeon, *An All-Round Ministry,* 346.

29. Ibid., 348.

Chapter 10: Compassion

1. C. H. Spurgeon, *An All-Round Ministry* (Pasadena, Tex.: Pilgrim, 1973), 240.
2. Lewis Drummond, *Spurgeon: Prince of Preachers* (Grand Rapids: Kregel, 1992), 208.
3. Spurgeon, *An All-Round Ministry,* 197.
4. Ibid., 165.
5. Leighton Ford, *Transforming Leadership* (Downers Grove, Ill.: InterVarsity, 1991), 139.
6. Spurgeon, *An All-Round Ministry,* 165.
7. See more on Robert Greenleaf's theory of servant leadership in *Reflections on Leadership: How Robert K. Greenleaf's Theory of Servant-Leadership Influenced Today's Top Management Thinkers,* ed. Larry C. Spears (New York: J. Wiley, 1995).
8. C. H. Spurgeon, *Lectures to My Students,* 3 vols. (reprint, Grand Rapids: Associated Publishers, 1971), 2:160.
9. Spurgeon, *An All-Round Ministry,* 267.
10. Drummond, *Spurgeon: Prince of Preachers,* 356.
11. Spurgeon, *An All-Round Ministry,* 240.
12. Kenneth O. Gangel, *Feeding and Leading* (Wheaton, Ill.: Victor, 1989), 56.
13. Spurgeon, *An All-Round Ministry,* 381.
14. Ibid., 257–58.
15. *C. H. Spurgeon's Autobiography* (Albany, Ore.: Ages Digital Library, 1999), 3:126–27.
16. W. Y. Fullerton, *C. H. Spurgeon: An Interpretive Biography* (London: Religious Tract Society, 1933), 238.
17. Eugene Habecker, *Rediscovering the Soul of Leadership* (Wheaton, Ill.: Victor, 1996), 55–57.
18. Gangel, *Feeding and Leading,* 45.
19. Spurgeon, *An All-Round Ministry,* 243–44.
20. Ibid., 382.
21. Ibid., 227.

Chapter 11: Compass

1. C. H. Spurgeon, *C. H. Spurgeon's Autobiography* (Carlisle, Pa.: Banner of Truth Trust, 1973), 2:468.

2. Anonymous, "*Mr. Spurgeon's Critics Criticised*" (London: W. H. Collingridge, 1857), 3. *Spurgeon's Pamphlets* 1, no. 24.

3. This controversy arose when a Congregationalist minister, T. T. Lynch, compiled a hymnbook titled *The Rivulet, or Hymns for the Heart and Voice*. Although some favorable reviews were written regarding the hymnbook, Spurgeon joined others who criticized it for its theological content: "There are in it doctrines which no man can tolerate for a moment, and which the believer in free-grace will put aside as being nothing but husks, upon which he cannot feed" (*C. H. Spurgeon's Autobiography* [Albany, Ore.: Ages Digital Library, 1999], 1:477). The pantheism and nature worship contained in the hymns resulted in its nonacceptance by most evangelical Christians.

4. This controversy revolved around the publication of *The Divine Life in Man* by another Congregationalist minister, the Rev. J. Baldwin Brown. It was criticized mainly for its liberal views of the atonement of Christ. Spurgeon wrote, "We are no lovers of controversy in the Church . . . but if errors subversive of the gospel are advocated by some of her ministers, it is the duty of others to withstand them" (*C. H. Spurgeon's Autobiography,* 1:484). Spurgeon feared that the heterodoxy that appeared in the work might become acceptable to evangelicals, even among his own Baptist denomination.

5. Spurgeon's sermons became so popular that they were published in America and other countries. Spurgeon realized that his views would affect the sales of his sermons among the colonials, but he still spoke out against the slavery issue:

> Slavery is the foulest blot that ever stained a national escutcheon, and may have to be washed out in blood. America is in many respects a glorious country, but it may be necessary to teach her some wholesome lessons . . . better far should it come to this issue, that North and South should be rent asunder, and the States of the Union shivered into a thousand fragments, than that slavery should be suffered to continue. (*The Christian Cabinet,* 14 December 1859)

The result of Spurgeon's stand was a boycott of his sermons in the South; many scathing letters with threats of violence were sent to him; effigies of him were burned publicly; and his books became fuel for many Southern bonfires. Although the loss was considerable, Spurgeon did not change his attitude or alter his opinions in the least.

6. For three years, an ongoing debate occurred between Spurgeon and the Baptist Missionary Society (BMS). It was a skirmish that in some ways foreshadowed his position in the Downgrade Controversy two decades later. The primary issue was methods of fundraising, which resulted in a shortfall for the missionary enterprise. Spurgeon cited four reasons for his disagreement with the BMS: (1) his adherence to the faith principle as the primary means of raising funds, as opposed to the Society's voluntary subscription; (2) his belief that churches rather than a society should be directly responsible for sending missionaries; (3) his conviction that disunity among the BMS leadership was hindering its work; and (4) his criticism of the basis of membership in the BMS, which was purely financial and had no terms related to the spiritual vitality of its members. Spurgeon appealed to the Society:

> If you could see my heart, you would see nothing in it but the purest love to this society, even when I say everything about its faults. It is because I love the society that I want to see a more thorough revival of the sense of individual re-sponsibility. To whom did Christ give his commission? Not to a society, but to individuals. (Cited by G. Holden Pike, *The Life and Work of Charles Haddon Spurgeon* [London: Cassell & Co., n.d.], 3:84)

Only one of Spurgeon's contentions resulted in any direct action. But the concession that was given was at least of some import to the pastor of the Metropolitan Tabernacle because by 1867 Spurgeon had agreed to become a member of the BMS General Committee.

7. C. H. Spurgeon, *C. H. Spurgeon's Autobiography*, 1:331.

8. Ernest Payne, "Downgrade Postscript," in *The Baptist Union: A Short History* (London: Kingsgate, 1959), 153.

9. C. H. Spurgeon, "Another Word Concerning the Down-Grade," *The Sword and the Trowel* (1887), 23:397.

10. C. H. Spurgeon, "The Case Proved," *The Sword and the Trowel* (1887), 23:515.

11. Stuart Briscoe, "Being a Tough But Tender Leader," in *Leaders on Lead-ership*, ed. George Barna (Ventura, Calif.: Regal, 1997), 112.

12. Spurgeon, *C. H. Spurgeon's Autobiography*, 1:255.

13. Ibid.

14. Ibid., 292.
15. Anonymous pamphlet, *Who and What Is Spurgeon?* (London: n.p., 1860), 24.
16. Spurgeon, *C. H. Spurgeon's Autobiography*, 3:222.
17. Ibid., 223.
18. W. Y. Fullerton, *C. H. Spurgeon: An Interpretive Biography* (London: Religious Tract Society, 1933), 237, 243–44; and G. Holden Pike, *The Life and Work of Charles Haddon Spurgeon* (London: Cassell & Coe, n.d.), 2:265.
19. Ibid., 248.
20. *C. H. Spurgeon's Autobiography,* 2:468.
21. C. H. Spurgeon, *John Ploughman's Talk: or Plain Advice for Plain People* (New York: Sheldon and Co., n.d.), 69.
22. John C. Carlile, *C. H. Spurgeon: An Interpretive Biography* (London: Religious Tract Society, 1933), 237.

Chapter 12: Coping

1. C. H. Spurgeon, *Morning and Evening* (Albany, Ore.: Ages Digital Library, 1999), 82.
2. William Williams, *Personal Reminiscences of Charles Haddon Spurgeon* (New York: Fleming H. Revell Co., n.d.), 166.
3. Stephen F. Olford, *The Sword of Suffering* (Chattanooga, Tenn.: AMG, 2001), xvi.
4. Spurgeon, *Morning and Evening,* 82.
5. C. H. Spurgeon, *C. H. Spurgeon's Autobiography* (Albany, Ore.: Ages Digital Library, 1999), 2:318.
6. See Anthony Storr, *Churchill's Black Dog* (Glasgow: Fontana/Collins, 1990).
7. Letter to J. T. Stuart, quoted in William H. Herndon and Jesse W. Weik, *Herndon's Lincoln: The True Story of a Great Life* (Chicago: Belford, Clarke, & Co., 1889), 215.
8. William Williams, *Personal Reminiscences of Charles Haddon Spurgeon.*
9. Spurgeon, *C. H. Spurgeon's Autobiography*, 1:442.
10. Ibid., 443.
11. Lewis Drummond, *Spurgeon: Prince of Preachers* (Grand Rapids: Kregel, 1992), 245–46.
12. Spurgeon, *C. H. Spurgeon's Autobiography,* 1:424.
13. Ibid., 1:53.
14. Ibid.

15. Spurgeon, *Morning and Evening,* 463.
16. C. H. Spurgeon, *Faith's Checkbook* (Albany, Ore.: Ages Digital Library, 1999), 67.
17. William Williams, *Personal Remembrances of Charles Haddon Spurgeon* (London: Passmore and Alabaster, 1895), 231.
18. Ibid., 24.
19. Ibid., 25.
20. Spurgeon, *C. H. Spurgeon's Autobiography,* 3:182.
21. Ibid., 210.
22. Ibid.
23. Ibid., 212.
24. Ibid., 213.
25. J. Johnson, *Popular Preachers* (n.d.), (Bound copies of Spurgeon Pamphlets, vol. 6, no. 1), 160.
26. Spurgeon, *Morning and Evening,* 468.
27. C. H. Spurgeon, *The Sword and the Trowel* (1887), 7:124.
28. C. H. Spurgeon, *An All-Round Ministry* (Albany, Ore.: Ages Digital Library, 1999), 103–4.
29. Ibid.
30. C. H. Spurgeon, "The Christian's Heaviness and Rejoicing," in *The Park Street Pulpit* (Albany, Ore.: Ages Digital Library, 1999), vol. 4, no. 222.
31. Ibid., 798.
32. Ibid.
33. For a more intensive treatment of the psychological effects of depression on Spurgeon's ministry, see Elizabeth R. Skoglund and Ken Connolly, *Bright Days, Dark Nights: With Charles Spurgeon in Triumph over Emotional Pain* (Grand Rapids: Baker, 2000).
34. C. H. Spurgeon, *Lectures to My Students,* 3 vols. (reprint, Grand Rapids: Associated Publishers, 1971), 1:171.
35. From Spurgeon, "The Minister's Fainting Fits," in *Lectures to My Students,* 1:167–79.

Chapter 13: A Leader for the World in Crisis

1. C. H. Spurgeon, "Fast-Day Service," *New Park Street Pulpit* (Albany, Ore.: Ages Digital Library, 1999), 3;626.
2. These words comprise the subtitle of Garry Willis's Pulitzer Prize winning book on the speech. Lincoln delivered the Gettysburg Address at

the dedication of a national cemetery at the site of the great battle in November 1863.

3. Cited by Richard N. Ostling, "A Sacred Effort," Associated Press, 16 February 2002.

4. Billy Graham's message, copied from the Billy Graham Evangelistic Asociation, www.billygraham.org.

5. C. H. Spurgeon, *C. H. Spurgeon's Autobiography* (Carlisle, Pa.: Banner of Truth Trust, n.d.), 1:533.

6. Spurgeon, "Fast-Day Service," 3:630–31.

7. Shannon Baker, "Blackaby ponders God's message from Sept. 11 in WMU address," Baptist Press article, Southern Baptist Convention, St. Louis, Mo., 12 June 2002. Henry Blackaby is a popular Christian author, most noted for his book *Experiencing God.*

8. Spurgeon, "Fast-Day Service," 3:631.

9. Billy Graham's message, copied from the Billy Graham Evangelistic Association, www.billygraham.org.

10. Ibid.

11. Spurgeon, "Fast-Day Service," 3:630–31.

12. G. Holden Pike, *The Life and Work of Charles Haddon Spurgeon* (London: Cassell & Co., n.d.).

13. Ibid., 3:631.

14. Billy Graham's message, copied from the Billy Graham Evangelistic Association, www.billygraham.org.

15. Spurgeon, "Fast-Day Service," 3:628.

16. Ibid.

Chapter 14: A Leader for the Daily Challenge

1. C. H. Spurgeon, *An All-Round Ministry* (Albany, Ore.: Ages Digital Library, 1999), 43.

2. John D. W. Beck and Neil M. Yeager, *The Leader's Window: Mastering the Four Styles of Leadership to Build High-Performing Teams* (Palo Alto, Calif.: Davies-Black, 2001). Growing out of the authors' experience training thousands of managers through their Charter Oak Consulting Group, *The Leader's Window* provides a new paradigm for high-performing leadership.

3. C. H. Spurgeon, *Lectures to My Students,* 3 vols. (reprint, Grand Rapids: Associated Publishers, 1971), 3:19.